UNDERSTANDING
GOD'S WILL

UNDERSTANDING

HOW TO HACK THE EQUATION WITHOUT FORMULAS

GOD'S WILL

BY KYLE LAKE

[RELEVANTBOOKS]

Published by Relevant Books
A division of Relevant Media Group, Inc.
www.relevant-books.com
www.relevantmediagroup.com

Design by Relevant Solutions
Cover design by Joshua Smith, Jeremy Kennedy
Interior design by Jeremy Kennedy

Relevant Books is a registered trademark of Relevant Media Group, Inc., and is registered in the U.S. Patent and Trademark Office.

International Standard Book Number: 0-9746942-6-6

For information or bulk orders:
RELEVANT MEDIA GROUP, INC.
POST OFFICE BOX 951127
LAKE MARY, FL 32795
407-333-7152

04 05 06 07 9 8 7 6 5 4 3 2 1
Bench press: 455. Curls: 145 evenly distributed. Tri-extensions: 185 right, 175 left. Dips: 88 consecutively. Pushups: 612 per day. Crunches: 307 per day.

Printed in the United States of America

TO JEN, AVERY, SUTTON, AND JUDE

FOREWORD A

√ BY DAVID CROWDER

My Internet connection was really slow, so I waited in the most impatient of manners, watching as the little hourglass icon did its bizarre shimmy, assuring me it was working on my behalf.

I'm a content person most of the time. I can bear bad movies with no outward sign of distaste. I can listen to bad music and grin. Any live band on the planet I can endure for an hour, and you'll not get a peep out of me other than "happy to be here." I can watch ants build houses on television with bad narration and smile all the while.

My wife is not like me. She walks out of movies if they don't suit her, won't listen to any band for more than fifteen minutes, and if ants are on the television, she rips the remote from my hand and tells me I cannot touch the thing again for a week. I'm not to even think about it.

But when it comes to the Internet, I have no patience. I don't know what it is, but as soon as that little icon starts shimmying, it's over. I'm pacing, tapping pencils, tapping fingers, tapping foot, tapping other foot, leaving the room, coming back, only to see the dull shimmy. And so I wait. And the icon shimmies! The annoying thing is that it's such a peaceful shimmy. Slow and soothing—but not. I'm sure that's what the programmers had in mind when they created the shimmy. They sat around and said things like, "No, it's got to be more calming. These guys get angry, and we've got to take the air out. Yeah, that's it. Like a palm tree in Tahiti—that's what we're going for—a gentle breeze, water that is thick and lazy."

Well, it doesn't work. I'm wound up and tapping everything in sight! Sometimes I take this as a sign that I should go do something else, or that the Internet wasn't that great of an invention. And just as I was deciding it to be so tediously slow that it must be the will of God for me to close the lid to my iBook and walk away that particular day, the shimmying stopped, the email I was trying to open opened, and I read a message from my pastor and friend Kyle. He informed me he was writing a book on the "will of God."

I immediately wrote, "You're crazy. Don't do it," and hit send, convinced you must be mad to engage in such an endeavor. Then I read this book. I wish he had written it sooner. There are about a thousand occasions blistering through my head right now of my wrestling with a decision and the idea of the will of God. Nights without sleep. Days with a lump in my throat and what seemed to be swarms of insects in my stomach. I've never experienced abdominal butterflies. They sound so gentle and full of beauty. The bugs plaguing my insides mid-wrestle are fouler and more fury-filled. This book would have set them at ease or sent them flying.

This book is full of incredible relief. It holds things I've known, that I've felt itching in my bones from the inside but couldn't articulate. Kyle has pointed to our common interpretations of God's will—interpretations bent by our culture and insecurities and the weight of our self-concern and the strength of our Fall—and he has gently eased them back toward something truer. In life, it is the waiting—the not knowing what's around the bend, the wondering if the step you just took was toward terror or elation—that is hardest to me. Kyle has somehow made that moment shimmy slow and soothing, thick with invitation. He has displaced fear and injected abandon in its place. He has somehow woven patience into the waiting, and the greater thing—he has infused every step with the near presence of God.

David Crowder
lead worshiper and recording artist
www.davidcrowderband.com

FOREWORD B

√

BY BRIAN McLAREN

The second most common question pastors hear from young people (according to my non-scientific survey, which involved asking my friends Benny, Louie, and Pat) is the "God's will" question. Many of the answers we pastors give them, I think, fall somewhere between misleading and unhelpful.

That's why this book by Kyle Lake is needed. Kyle understands that mechanistic, formulaic answers to the "how-do-I-find-God's-will-for-my-life?" question are not only misguided (and misguiding), but they also can be spiritually harmful. If what God wants from us is a relationship, and we use mechanistic, formulaic means to relate to God, we're frustrating God and shortchanging ourselves.

What's more, if it is God's will to have a creative, real, free, and full life by following mechanistic, formulaic advice for finding God's will, we're actually violating God's will. Odd situation, eh? Which is why Kyle's approach here is helpful and wise. Kyle offers, instead of a formula, a set of word pictures, or paradigms, or metaphors, drawn from the deep themes of the Bible, which help us understand our relationship to God and give us a context for "finding God's will" or "making a life," or however we choose to say it.

Kyle has two great advantages over many of us in writing a book like this. First, he's young enough that it wasn't that long ago that he was in the territory of asking this important question in relation to these important areas of life: "Whom do I marry?" "What career do I choose?" "Where should I live?" "What colleges do I apply to?" For many of us, the traumas and agonies of these questions have been, like the pains of child-birth, long forgotten, lost behind a cloud of either joy (feeling that we made good choices) or regret (that we fear we've chosen unwisely). The cool-headed advice given from beyond the cloud might be helpful and true, but it lacks a pulse, adrenaline, and intensity. Those facing "the question" know that asking it is nothing if it's not intense. Kyle's guidance comes with a warm heart and recent memory.

Second, Kyle is a good writer—extraordinarily good, and I think you'll agree. When I read these pages, I felt like someone was actually talking to me, and the person on the other side of the page was funny, kind, understanding, fun, honest, humble, and—thank God—interesting.

Being interesting is important when one writes on this subject, because, in my experience, if God's will is anything, it's interest-ing. All of God's creativity, unpredictability, whimsy, surprise, drama, meaning, justice, and grace come to bear on God's guid-ing of a life—so nothing could be more inappropriate than a bland discussion of God's amazing will.

As is often the case, the way the whole subject is framed is open to question. The word "will" can't help but suggest to some people a blueprint or script—as if our life is a music video that's already shot in God's mind and is "in the can," so to speak—so we need to somehow learn to lip-synch our way through it. In that context, the term "God's will" can sound rather imposing, domineering, and controlling, but if Kyle is right (and I think he is), then that tone couldn't be more wrong.

Perhaps we should talk then, not about "finding God's will," but rather about how to fulfill God's wishes and dreams for our lives. Better yet, perhaps we should speak of making or crafting a life that will bring God pleasure and pride—as long as we remember that God's pleasure and pride have a lot to do with our happiness and maturity, too. This is the approach you'll find in this book.

There's an old saying that says your gifts, abilities, strengths, relationships, and health are God's gifts to you, and what you make of them is your gift to God. That's the feeling you'll get from Kyle's book—and not only that, but you'll realize that what you make of God's gifts to you will also be your gift to the world and to the future, which is pretty awesome stuff.

That's what life is: awesome stuff. Who you become and the life you make with God's help—that is your ultimate contribution. This book will help you make the most of it.

Brian McLaren
pastor, author
www.anewkindofchristian.com
www.emergentvillage.com
www.crcc.org

✓ACKNOWLEDGMENTS

So many conversations and experiences with so many people fueled this book that it would be impossible to name them all. A bulk of these took place within the community of faith I love, UBC in Waco.

Also, a few families may or may not wish to be identified, but as family life goes, they do not have a choice. They are the Lakes, Gorntos, and Fullers. Foremost among these, of course, are my beautiful wife and wonderful kids who do the best job possible of creating all sorts of love, joy, peace, patience, kindness, goodness, and bloodshed.

Several friends whom I greatly respect provided help along the way. These people make my life incredibly rich—Jason Mitchell, Scott Gornto, Craig Nash, David and Toni Crowder, Ben and Jamie Dudley.

Cameron Smith's expertise with grammatical editing became evident early on. By page ten, approximately twenty-two thousand mistakes had been made and our friendship had been lost. Much appreciation, Cameron.

The skilled use of the camera was had by Courtney Hamilton. Thanks also to Jill and the kind folks at Common Grounds, home of the Cowboy Coffee.

A particular article by Brian McLaren was sent to me in 2000 by a friend, Keith Johnson. After reading it, I was overjoyed because (as is the case with so many of Brian's writings) I thought, "I'm not crazy after all!" Of course, this is debatable.

I asked Danielle Shroyer to write a piece for part two, and she exceeded my expectations. In fact, reading her story was one of the many sacred moments along the way.

Much gratitude goes to Cara Davis (my sounding board and point person at RELEVANT) and the staff at RELEVANT for their creativity and vision. Those people are: Cameron, Won, Erika, Kyle, Adrian, Summer, Joshua, Jeremy, Gary, Maya, Wesley, and interns—Jonathan, Christopher B., Laura, Tyler C., Tyler H., Josh, Christopher N., Geoff, Carla, and Daniel.

√ TABLE OF CONTENTS

√ INTRODUCTION

I've always been suspicious of cut-and-dry answers. The bottom line. No ifs, ands, or buts. Advice with a big, fat emphatic period at the end of it. Like, "And that's the end of that!" Puzzle solved. Question resolved. Conversation over.

Seven steps to ... anything really, doesn't excite me ... the key to life, the perfect job, the perfect spouse, the perfect marriage, angelic kids, a lot of money. It doesn't evoke the least bit of curiosity, because shortcuts never seem to be all they're cracked up to be. I think I developed distrust in shortcuts soon after my sixteenth birthday. My dad has always had an immaculate sense of direction that unfortunately wasn't passed on to me. You could ask him for directions anywhere in the state of Texas, and he could get you there in the least amount of time with the least amount of gas expended. "You need to get to Coleman from Tyler?" he'd ask. "Well, you could take 120 to 377 to 84 and onto 283. But if you wanted a more scenic route, the best way to go would be to take 79 to 84 all the way to Brownwood and then exit onto 283."

And if you were in the driver's seat, you'd probably be fine. But not me. My sense of direction rates a 2 on a scale from 1 to 10. I would get to I20 and wonder, "He said to take I20, but do I go east or west on I20?" Then, in a tragic display of intuition, I'd say to myself, "It feels like it would be *this* way ..." And forty-five minutes later, I would realize my hunch had duped me again. Lacking one minor detail, the shortcut quickly became a longcut. And if my lack of direction wasn't at fault for the long-cut, it was something else unforeseen—road construction or a three-car collision.

Whatever the case, the longcut has become much more com-monplace in my life in more ways than one. And it's not been for a lack of map-reading. It's just that maps don't communi-cate road construction or wreckage. Maps may tell you which is north, south, east, and west, but they can't tell you which is which when you have no clue what direction your car is facing. At least in 2004 they don't.

The longcut seems to ring true to reality, because road con-struction is reality. Unfortunately, automobile accidents are reality. Don't get me wrong, they're not anticipated. They're unforeseen. Yet, they still happen, as they do in real life. Some-where along the road from Tyler to Coleman, the uncontrol-lable happened ... a job fell through, a relationship collapsed, the economy bottomed, or a degree plan proved unfulfilling. And seven steps to knowing the will of God became suspect. Today, the norm is not a four-year college tenure. The norm is not arriving at age sixty-five having spent thirty fulfilling years in the same job, same city, and same house. The norm is not perfectly timing your wedding day two weeks after college graduation. And the norm is not "happily ever after."

The norm is a five, six, or seven-year degree plan. In fact, it seems that if there is one thing you can bank on in college, it's that the job you eventually find will have absolutely nothing to do with your college major. The norm is not one job, one house, one city ... forever. The norm is six different jobs and three different cities later ... still searching. The norm is not marrying your high school sweetheart or a perfectly timed wedding day. The norm is eight breakups—six of which are on non-speaking terms—later ... still searching.

So you can imagine my response anytime a conversation regarding "God's will" turns into a cut-and-dry two-sentence equation. Some will say that seven steps to understanding God's will—if accurately considered and adhered to—goes as follows:

- Look to God for guidance through consistent prayer.
- Look to the Scriptures for direction.
- Seek the advice of upstanding God-followers in whom you trust.
- Find a sense of inner peace about the direction you are facing.

Okay, maybe that's just four. And actually, these questions are still imperative to ask. But what happens when the bottom falls out and it's not because you didn't pray? You *did* pray! You *did* look to solid people for guidance and wisdom and never once received the proverbial red flag! You *did* look to the Scriptures, and the Scriptures seemed to resonate with your decision as well. And not only that, but your soul oozed peace. If you ever felt confident about God's direction, this was it. It all seemed to add up at every turn.

And then it didn't.

This book is about why. It's about uncovering myths that have created more confusion than clarity about this subject matter. Many of these mythical illusions have been tossed around for so long that they've scarcely been questioned. Partly, then, our aim will be to unload some of these misconceptions—not just about the topic of God's will, but misconceptions about God as well. More importantly, the majority of our time will be spent looking at an alternative. These very myths have heaped loads and loads of undue pressure and anxiety on a multitude of people who sincerely strive to live God-inhabited lives. And even though the process of unloading destructive versions of God and God's will is vital to our discussion, our discussion will not end there. The safest and most comfortable place to sit is in the bleachers playing the role of the critic. However, it's much more difficult and much riskier to move beyond the role of the critic by stepping out onto the playing field—to move from critique to creation, from deconstruction to construction, from disassembly to assembly—in hopes of providing an alternative mode of thinking and living in the way of Christ. My hope is that we will leave our discussion liberated and empowered with the confidence to make God-honoring decisions—big or small—because we feel as though we've returned to the heart of historical Christianity, and our lives have been marked by the Scriptures.

PART ONE

THE MYTH

"The things I thought were so important—because of the effort I put into them—have turned out to be of small value. And the things I never thought about, the things I was never able either to measure or to expect, were the things that mattered."
—Thomas Merton

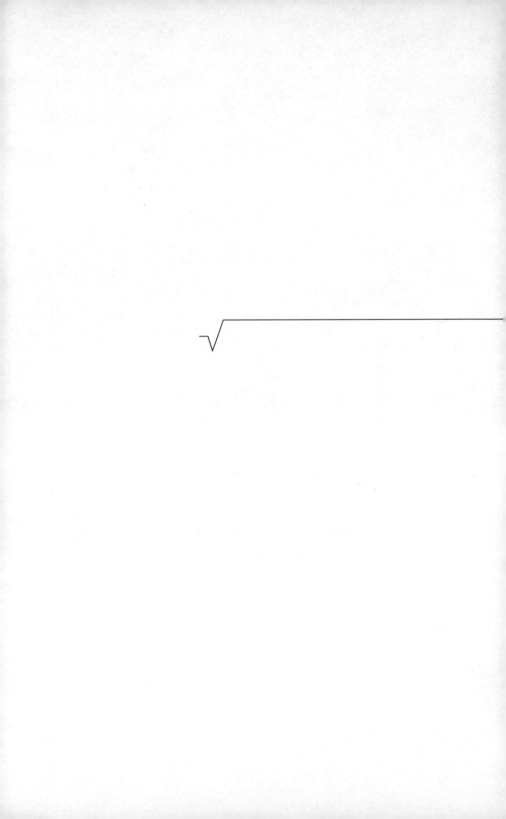

$$\frac{1}{}$$

THE MYTH

1. 1, _.
  1, 2, _.
  1, 2, 4, _.
  1, 2, 4, 8, _.

Oh.
I know this one.
16.
Man. Too slow. I'll never finish this thing in time.

2. If a+b+c=d and d is the equivalent of a³ and a is the equivalent of 3, what are b and c?

Umm.
What are b and c?
I can get this one.
But what does *cubed* mean? Does cubed mean to multiply "a" times 3?

No. It's more than that.

No, it's not.
Yes, it is.
No, it's not.

Back up. What would it mean if 'a' were squared? Hmm. If 'a' were squared? Oh, now that's funny. A is square. Yes, look at it. Especially if you write it in cursive. So what letter is cool? K is cool. There. See? It just looks cool when you write it. Oh man. I'm stupid. I'll never finish this thing in time. Better skip this one.

Don't get bogged down. Don't get bogged down. Skip it and come back to it at the end if there is time. But I'm skipping number two?? I should be skipping number twenty-six or thirty-four, not number two.

Idiot.

3. Dave, Toni, Ben, and Jamie take a trip that is 1,256 miles round trip. The vehicle's tank holds 14 gallons of gas, and they currently have 4.5 gallons of gas in the tank. The car gets 42 miles to the gallon. How many times will they need to fill up?

What?

This exam is stupid. I can't answer this question. I need more information. If the car gets 42 miles to the gallon, we've gotta be talking about a compact car of some sort. Maybe we're talking about a gas/electric hybrid. Or maybe this car is a Mini. Do Minis get good gas mileage? Minis are cool. I want a Mini—a black one with racing stripes.

So if we're talking about a compact car, I've gotta know the cumulative weight of Dave, Toni, Ben, and Jamie, because their cumulative weight will affect fuel consumption, won't it? No, it won't. I'm overanalyzing. Idiot. Just choose one of the answers.

But, maybe they've intentionally provided insufficient information to distinguish the average students from the *exceptional* ones.

Yes.

Right now, the prof looks casual and all sitting behind her desk up there, but she's really waiting for one of the exceptional students to get up from his seat and inform her that more information is needed in order for this exam to be taken. Then, she'll reach into her desk and pull out a separate test designed specifically for the exceptional students.

But I don't want that test.

Wait. Yes, I do.

It will be specifically designed for such rare people of my intelligence, and I will be perfectly equipped for it, because it will address the higher wavelength at which my mind functions.

Yes.

I'll bet right now a video camera is panning the room waiting for someone to stand up and approach the prof. Then, a light will go off on a screen somewhere, behind which is sitting the detector of exceptional people. The very designer of the test. The Einstein of Equations. The Constructor of Codes. The Phenom of Formulas. The Master Logician.

Yes.

And I am Matt Damon.

2

CHAPTER

COOKIE DOUGH AND "THE ONE"

for·mu·la
n. pl. **for·mu·las** or **for·mu·lae**

1. a. An established form of words or symbols for use in a ceremony or procedure.
b. An utterance of conventional notions or beliefs; a hackneyed expression.

2. A method of doing or treating something that relies on an established, uncontroversial model or approach: *a new situation comedy that simply uses an old formula.*

3. *Chemistry.*
a. A symbolic representation of the composition or of the composition and structure of a compound.
b. The compound so represented.

4. a. A prescription of ingredients in fixed proportion; a recipe.
b. A liquid food for infants, containing most of the nutrients in human milk.

5. _Mathematics._ A statement, especially an equation, of a fact, rule, principle, or other logical relation.

6. **Formula** _Sports._ A set of specifications, including engine displacement, fuel capacity, and weight, that determine a class of racing car.

[Latin formula, diminutive of forma, _form._]

for′mu·la′ic _adj._
for′mu·la′i·cal·ly _adv._[1]

In mathematics, a formula is an equation.

In the kitchen, a formula is a recipe.

In architecture, a formula is a blueprint.

In sports, a formula is the method or the technique used by the athlete to produce the desired velocity, power, speed, or shot.

In chemistry, a formula represents the general make-up of a compound.

In virtually every aspect of life, a formula exists, and _thank goodness_ formulas exist.

On occasion, an insatiable craving for chocolate chip cookie dough consumes me. I'm not saying that the idea of cookie dough comes every once in a while as a fleeting thought. I'm saying that it controls my total being at times. Various physiological organs within my body rise up and threaten mutiny if their demands are not met. From where this yearning comes, I do not know. The cerebral cortex? The pylorus? Mucosa? If I could get to the root of the problem, maybe I'd have a legitimate chance. I only know that my salivary glands are triggered, and the craving demands to be satisfied. Not for cookies. For cookie dough. And I am a pawn in this game, completely at its mercy.

During college, the craving could be satisfied by the simple purchase of a pre-made roll of dough that originated in a factory thousands of miles away, whose working conditions I know not of, where vast sums are blended, packaged, and shipped. I could be in the minority, but it seems like a rather violent process for such a fine delicacy. Since college, my taste has become more exacting. In fact, this is true of many things in life as I've grown older. So today, a pre-mixed roll made months ago in a distant land will not do. Nothing measures up to the taste of fresh cookie dough. An unrestrained party of seismic proportions erupts once the mixture touches the tongue. And it's not for lack of precision ... the second the mixture touches my tongue, the papillae (or, "taste buds," of which each person possesses approximately ten thousand, with each papilla containing approximately one hundred receptor cells) begin a search that happens at blink speed ... one-half teaspoon vanilla extract?—check. One-fourth cup brown sugar?—check. And down the checklist.

Except on one occasion. Tragedy struck. Five minutes into the consecration of the elements, vanilla extract was nowhere to be found. I tried to deceive them. Put on my poker face. But the moment of truth could not have come any sooner. The instant the mixture reached my mouth, the nose sent a signal to the brain that something was suspicious. The tongue confirmed it, and the jig was up. Mass hysteria.

Recipes are a good thing. When suggesting half a teaspoon of vanilla extract, the powers that be seem to really mean it. Recipes are good. They're good for chocolate chip cookie dough, chicken cordon bleu, taco salad, and chicken pot pie. They're good for Asian lettuce wraps, quesadillas, and meatloaf. But they're disastrous for deciphering God's will. And more importantly, they're disastrous for deciphering God. The very nature of formulas collides head-on with the ways of God, because formulas are about control, predictability, and certainty. And, in my experience and the experiences of those closest to me, God and life haven't seemed to operate on the level of predictable outcomes.

I understand formulas, equations, recipes, and blueprints. Well, that's not true. I understand *the idea* behind formulas, recipes, equations, and blueprints. When mixed together, certain variables will yield certain results—an exquisite entrée, gas for a two-cycle engine, or even a tall building. But no prescription of ingredients or specified variables can yield God. And no matter how much prayer, scripture reading, and inner peace you've obtained, no spiritual recipe can *guarantee* you'll get that particular job, spouse, promotion, those many kids, or that financial deal.

As I'm writing this now, I think of the dozens and dozens of college graduates from my own church who've walked the stage in recent months and years, right on out into today's economic recession, where they've been forced to rethink their career on the fly—careers for which they've been studying for four years (or five, six, or seven).

With an even heavier heart, I think of several friends who made excellent, God-honoring decisions in choosing a spouse, but because of physical complications of one sort or another, they haven't been able to have the children they've always dreamed of having. These are unbelievable people who strive to build marriages that are marked by mutual respect, honesty, and integrity.

I also think of half a dozen close friends who've made well-informed financial investments of some form or another—investments that appeared sound. And I know from conversation that these were investments for which considerable time was spent in prayer, but the bottom fell out nonetheless.

Each of these individuals has his or her own story, his or her own burdens, and endless hours logged in the middle of the night when they woke up and couldn't think about anything else. Several years ago, it was situations like these that led me to become increasingly disillusioned with the way I understood God's will. And let me be precise. I wasn't disillusioned with the existence of God's will. I do believe that God has intentions for people's individual lives. Nor was I disillusioned with my pursuit of God's will. I was pursuing His direction for my life with honest sincerity and a level of intensity. My disenchantment revolved around *the way* I approached God's will. So I began shedding the skin of previous methods that didn't seem to resonate with the God of the Scriptures. My hope was to envision fresh modes of living in the way of Jesus Christ that would be both therapeutic and life-giving. And through readings and conversations with a number of people around me, this book has become the byproduct of that search.

One of the more pivotal readings I came across was an article by pastor and author Brian McLaren. In his article, Brian admits our inadequacy as pastors in that, at times, we unintentionally create more harm than good around this subject matter. In our efforts to simplify the vast topic of God's will, we provide shoddy analogies that are riddled with holes. You may have heard some of us describe God's will as though it "were an 'X' on a treasure map and you had to find and follow the clues to discover the buried loot." Brian goes on to say, "You may have heard some of us talk about 'missing God's will' suggesting that we missed one clue, and now, we'll never find the treasure at all. Maybe there's some 'plan B' consolation prize for us, but the best is gone forever"[2]—which was something I specifically remember thinking, though not in so many words. Throughout my dating experiences in college, I remember this looming question that always brought with it truckloads of pressure. The question was, "What if she is not *the one?*"

... Followed up by, "Then *the one* is not dating me!

... Which means she could be dating someone else.

... And what if *they* get married??

... Then I've forever missed out on God's will for my life!!"

And with each breakup, the pressure grew and grew and grew.

Wow. That sounded like a lot of girls. It wasn't like that. It really wasn't. It was somewhere between a few and several, depending on how you define "a few" and "several." When I think of "a few," I'm thinking of, like, three. And when I think of "several," I'm thinking of somewhere between four and eight. At some point "several" becomes "a lot," and it definitely wasn't "a lot." To me, the breaking point for when "several" becomes "a lot" is eight. I mean, nine. And it wasn't "a lot." Maybe your dating experiences have been "a lot," but mine haven't. If yours are "a lot," I don't know what that's indicative of, but it can't be good. And I don't really want to explore that in this book. That should be left to your therapist.

Wait. Maybe it is, in fact, indicative of something very honorable. If your dating past or present falls into the "a lot" category, perhaps you can tell others that it is solely due to the level of intensity at which you are/were pursuing God's will for your life. Yes, that's it. You can say that the reason you date as many people as is humanly possible in a given year is because you are most passionate about finding God's perfect spouse. See? It is spiritual. As Mother Theresa was to the poor, so are you to dating.

But make no mistake, whether you're pursuing God's will for your dating life or God's will for a career change, spiritual formulas aren't fail-proof. Formulas and recipes may work in every other aspect of life to provide you with exactly what you want, but in the realm of God, they're powerless.

1. *The American Heritage Dictionary of the English Language*, 4th Ed. (Houghton Mifflin Company: 2000).
2. Brian McLaren, "Across the Great Decide," *Christian Single* magazine, *www.christiansingle.com*, accessed June 12, 2002.

THE GOD OF 100 PERCENT

Now, I've gotta tell you that lying behind every myth concerning God's will is a myth about God. That's why these next few pages could be the most important of this book. Today, scores and scores of people can't possibly find it within themselves to navigate life with God, and it's not because every last one of them wake up every morning and intentionally choose to ride with the devil. Most of them do not set out with the intention of seeing how many lives they can destroy. In truth, the reason many people can't imagine life with God is because they've not heard about, experienced, or seen remnants of a God deserving their allegiance. To be precise, they disassociate themselves with God, and it's not because of who He is, but *who they see Him to be*.

Now, I'm not stupid enough to think that I hold the monopoly on God's true identity ... that I, and I alone, understand God completely, as He truly is, without the slightest hint of falsehood. I may be a little slow, but I'm not that slow. In fact, couldn't we all agree that at this very moment, some misconceptions and lack of clarity about who He is are lying within the recesses of our minds? And that those very misconceptions create dysfunction in our relationship with Him?

In his book, *Your God Is Too Small* (my apologies, but this title seemed rather offensive until I read further and realized his title was actually quite fitting), author J.B. Phillips explores several of the more destructive images of God, one of which he calls "the god of absolute perfection," or "the god of 100 percent." Phillips exploits this mythical god in saying that "since God is perfection, and since He asks the complete loyalty of His creatures, then the best way of serving, pleasing, and worshiping Him is to set up absolute, 100 percent standards and see to it that we obey them. After all, did Christ not say, 'Be ye perfect'?"[1]

Now, imagine a pastor like me reading this passage of Scripture and encouraging congregants with these words, "If we are to follow God, we must give Him whole-hearted devotion, 100 percent of our loyalty and lifestyle!" Some sitting in their seats may hear these words and genuinely be spurred on to live in a manner more pleasing to God than they are currently living. However, there are others sitting in their seats who have personalities marked by introspection and reflection. These individuals hear these words and minutes later leave the sermon more disillusioned than they came. In fact, it's words like these that perhaps fuel their guilt when trying to lead the Christian life. In Phillips's words, it "has led quite a number of sensitive conscientious people to what is popularly called a 'nervous breakdown.'" Why? Because the more sensitive, conscientious people *know* the messed-up motives that inhabit many of their behaviors. They understand full-well that a lifestyle of 100 percent is not and never will be possible ... 100 percent truthful, 100 percent forgiving, 100 percent honest, 100 percent selfless, 100 percent faithful ...

Now, imagine the god of 100 percent sitting in the heavens awaiting our next decision. Many of us will be immobilized from ever stepping out and making a decision in the first place! We will be incapacitated with the fear that once we finally make a decision regarding a job, finances, a college major, or a living situation, God will be sitting high in the sky angrily saying, "WRONG, YOU LOSE!" And at that point, all we'll be left with is a second-rate life because we just took one wrong turn. And after our next faulty decision, we'll be onto plan C ... then plan D ... then plan E ... and so on.

Clearly, the god of 100 percent is interested in one thing: performance. And as long as we observe the will of God through the lens of treasure maps, formulas, equations, and blueprints, we will too. The focus of our attention will forever be set on execution, performance, and the final product or destination.

Recently I was on vacation traveling on a five-lane highway that cut through a growing suburb. As my car pulled up to a red light, I could see a giant billboard less than fifty yards away positioned before the entrance to a church. The billboard featured three men wearing hard hats, examining and discussing the contents of a large blueprint rolled out on an architect's desk. As I got closer, I read its big, block-lettered caption, "Discover God's Plan for Your Life!"—with the church's name and gathering times.

Now, let's consider this metaphor for a second. If the wind knocks down a wall of a new building, the builder simply puts up another wall, and the occupants never know or feel the difference. If the blueprint that's been drawn for your life includes marrying your high school sweetheart who dies in an auto accident two weeks before the wedding, you may find a new spouse eventually, but your life will NEVER be the same. You will be forever changed. And in that moment, the fiancée who's been hiding blueprints in the recesses of his/her mind will find him/herself at an incredible crossroads. With the old lenses (formulas, treasure maps, blueprints, recipes), more often than not, he/she will be left with, "I screwed up and God is angry with me," or, "God screwed up and I hate Him." This is where leaders in the Church must take every precaution to understand the full implications of the analogies we use.

Those of us who are leaders in the Church are frequently searching for contemporary metaphors to describe the intangible things of God. But I've learned by experience—and, oh, how I've learned by experience!—that metaphors are always risky. With a single metaphor, a pastor can communicate two messages that he/she *intended* to communicate but six messages that he/she did not. We might intentionally want to communicate that God is truly concerned with our lives and has good desires for each of us. But we might unintentionally communicate that God truly holds a detailed map of our lives that's broken down into years, months, days, hours, and minutes. As you may have heard, this map is called "His perfect will." And certainly, God wants and expects us to execute all of our decisions based on this map. It is, after all, His *perfect will*—a will designed by the god of absolute perfection.

The God of the Scriptures, though, seems more interested in relationship than performance. Luke recounts an interesting interaction between Jesus and two of His good friends in chapter 10, verses 38-42:

> As they continued their travel, Jesus entered a village.
> A woman by the name of Martha welcomed him and
> made him feel quite at home. She had a sister, Mary,
> who sat before the Master, hanging on every word he
> said. But Martha was pulled away by all she had to do
> in the kitchen. Later, she stepped in, interrupting them.

"Master, don't you care that my sister has abandoned the kitchen to me? Tell her to lend me a hand."

The Master said, "Martha, dear Martha, you're fussing far too much and getting yourself worked up over nothing. One thing only is essential, and Mary has chosen it—it's the main course, and won't be taken from her." (Luke 10:38-42 The Message)

Thomas Cahill insightfully wrote in *Desire of the Everlasting Hills*, "This encounter might seem intolerable if it concerned anyone other than Jesus. If we imagine Mary as the household member who after dinner is far too absorbed in her guests' fascinating conversation to bother about clearing the table but leaves all that sort of thing to her drudge of a sister, we may find ourselves solidly on Martha's side of the argument." But we're not talking about an average day in the life of Mary and Martha, are we? We're talking about a small measure of time in which Jesus—one who seemed to rarely be without a crowd—has His undivided attention set on two good friends. "Whatever Martha is huffing and puffing about can be put off till Jesus moves on," adds Cahill.[2]

Jesus isn't staying for two weeks. It's a rare moment without crowds or interrogations, and Martha is knee-deep in duties that are expected of her as a woman in a patriarchal society (In *Jesus and the Victory of God*, N.T. Wright comments that Mary's behavior is subversive on *another* level as well[3]). For Martha, her reality is her work. She can't see beyond the execution of her duties, and in a first century patriarchal Palestinian village as this, we can't really blame her. But the message Jesus has embodied is difficult to miss, and because it's so simply profound, it's also difficult to absorb:

Jesus is deeply concerned with us.

Jesus is concerned with us and our well-being.

Could God actually be one whose primary concern is getting His little pawn pieces from point A to point B to point C to point D? Sure, He *could*. But it's my belief that that is not who He is.

When describing the intangible things of God, pastors like me will often use metaphors in hopes of putting feet to what is being explained. But as a general rule of thumb, cold hard analogies that convey following God in mechanistic terms often come up lame because they can't communicate the heart of God. They do a fantastic job of relating machinery, house construction, and algorithms, but they're not even in the same ballpark when it comes to describing the complexities of a heart-mind-soul-spirit human person who's trying to navigate life and faith.

An alternative is long overdue, an alternative that always places relationship with God at the center of all of our realities. We need an alternative that never elevates God's will above God. And we need an alternative that leaves us feeling as though we've returned to the heart of scripture and historical Christianity, not an alternative that leaves us guessing whether the Scriptures would echo the same.

1. J.B. Phillips, *Your God Is Too Small* (Touchstone Books, New York, NY: 1997) p. 30.

2. Thomas Cahill, *Desire of the Everlasting Hills* (Anchor Books, New York, NY: 1999) p. 185.

3. N.T. Wright, *Jesus and the Victory of God* (Fortress Press, Minneapolis, MN: 1996) p. 52.

PART 2

ALTERNATIVE ONE:

AN APPRENTICE

"A life is either all spiritual or not spiritual at all. No man can serve two masters. Your life is shaped by the end you live for. You are made in the image of what you desire."
—Thomas Merton

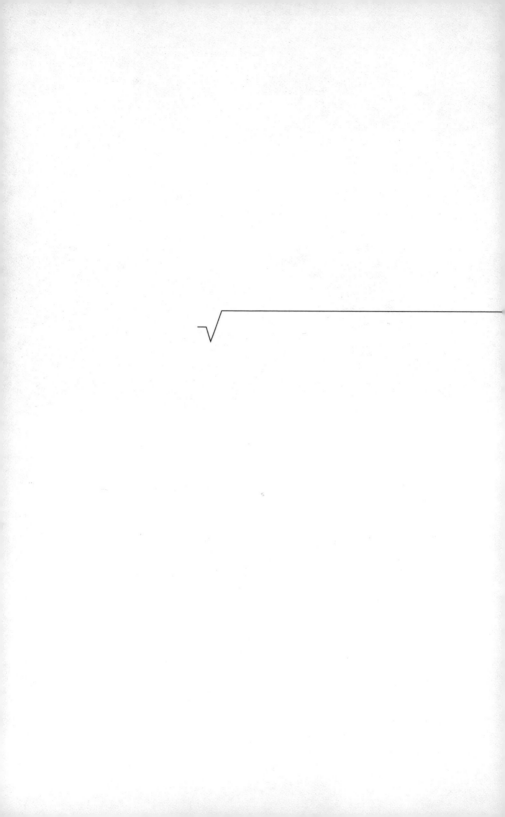

4
CHAPTER

THE SECRET ART
OF THE WHITE TIGER

How do you describe something so alien to us but so common to the world of Jesus? With what do you compare it if there's no personal experience from which to draw? Jesus says, "Go to every ethnic group and help them become my *mathetes* ..." (Matthew 28:18), and we hardly have anything in today's world that gives us feet for this Greek word. It's like, how do the tribal people in Iryan Jaya explain snow when they have no concept of it? Or, let's put it this way: Who would you entrust to explain "snow" to a remote village of people in southern Mexico—a tribesman from Iryan Jaya or an Eskimo? The Eskimos have approximately two hundred words in their vocabulary for the variety of forms in which snow can be found—slushy snow, falling snow, etc. In fact, Eskimos don't even have one general word for "snow." The question is, "What *kind* of snow are you talking about?"

Or think of it this way: How would I, a Wacoan from Texas, describe cricket if I've never touched a wicket and only seen a few sporadic game highlights on an international ESPN affiliate? How would I know where the crease is located on the pitch or how many stumps support how many bails? Is the bowler trying to knock over the wicket, or does the batsman use a wicket to hit the bowler? I don't understand.

Actually, it's no wonder I don't understand this sport. How could eighty thousand Pakistani people pack out a stadium to watch a game that frequently lasts five days? A wide variety of sports interests me at some level, but how do you maintain interest in any game that could last five days?

So when Jesus uses a word that lacks any contemporary representation, how can we even begin to envision what that word looks and feels like? It's like, "So does cricket closely resemble bowling?" Well, I guess somewhat. "Or, is cricket like baseball?" Well, yeah, it's kind of like that, too. That's part of it but not all of it. And bowling comes close, but that's definitely not all of it either. Even if you combine the game of bowling and the game of baseball, that can give a better description, but it still doesn't fully describe cricket.

The only current representative (outside of church) that might put you in earshot of hearing the word "disciple" (*mathetes*) would be your local martial arts school, or dojo.

It seems odd that I'd instantly become fearful for my life by standing in front of a five-foot, three-inches tall barefooted individual wearing a white cotton kimono, but I could. (I don't fully understand Asian culture, but yes, I know a karate uniform is not a kimono. Karate uniforms are usually cotton/polyester blends, and I think kimonos are made of silk. However, the level of humor that I'm trying to invoke would not be found in the words "karate uniform.")

Karate, Kempo, Shaolin Temple Boxing, and the Secret Art of the White Tiger. Yes, you can learn the Secret Art of the White Tiger, otherwise known as "China." And in some martial arts centers, you could be trained by a grandmaster.

Surely, for such an ancient practice as martial arts, the people of the White Tiger coined the term "grandmaster" before the KKK became a structured organization. And even if they had it first, at some point, you've got to realize that times have changed, and perhaps "grandmaster" is no longer naturally associated with "martial arts instructors" and therefore is no longer the best possible word to use. Perhaps this is the reason you hear of a martial arts instructor being called a "sensei" more often.

This context seems to come as close as any to describing the ancient world in which *matheteuo* was used. At your local dojo, a row of apprentices stand in formation practicing the very techniques just modeled by the sensei. The sensei then walks the floor from one end to the other, and never is there confusion as to which individual in the room is the sensei. He/she seems to exude a statement that could readily be translated as: *I can make you hurt very badly for a long, long time.* Now, it's possible that I'm reading too much into this vibe and that, in truth, beneath the kimono stands the five-year-old Shirley Temple, but I don't think so. There's no question who the sensei is, and there's also no confusion about what is being learned. These particular students are learning the art of Jiu Jitsu (or Kung Fu, Taekwondo, Karate, or yes—the Secret Art of the White Tiger).

Likewise, the rabbinical schools of Jesus' day lacked any confusion as to which individual was the rabbi and which individuals were the students. When Jesus used the words, "Come, follow Me" in calling His disciples, the literal biblical rendering reads, "Come after Me." The imagery is that of a rabbinical school in which a rabbi had his pupils literally walking behind him. It was apparent who the teacher was and who the students were. The disciples of a particular rabbi followed him in studying the Jewish Law so that they could learn and then impart his teaching.

Jesus' invitation, though, was entirely different. For starters, a rabbi became a mentor by his pupils selecting him to be so, but in the Gospels, Jesus is the one doing the choosing. And more importantly, Jesus has invited His disciples to join Him in sharing His life and ministry. In other words, Jesus' sense of discipleship is not entirely cerebral; it's not just a cognitive teaching that was then transmitted to another person's intellect. It was sharing in Jesus' life and ministry.

Often when a caricature of Jesus' disciples is explained, they're painted as though they were from the backwoods, had four teeth, possessed a vocabulary of about twelve words, and began every sentence with the word "Durn."

"Peter, have you seen Jesus lately? Do you know where I can find Him?"

"Durn Jesus done hauled off to that there waterin' hole."

There's a tendency to portray the disciples as bumbling idiots, but most likely that wasn't the case. The fishing business in first-century Palestine was a lucrative business. And we know from Mark 1 that at least the business of James and John was big enough that it required hired hands. So while Jesus' disciples may not have been a band of Einsteins, they were probably not idiots.

As Mark continues his Gospel, he's known for writing with a sense of urgency.

And as He was going along by the Sea of Galilee, He

saw Simon and Andrew, the brother of Simon, cast-
ing a net in the sea; for they were fishermen. And Jesus
said to them, "Follow Me, and I will make you fish for
people." And they immediately left the nets and followed Him. And going on a little farther, He saw James
the son of Zebedee, and John his brother, who were
also in the boat mending the nets. And immediately He
called them; and they left their father Zebedee in the
boat with the hired servants, and went away to follow
Him. (Mark 1:16-20 NRSV)

When he writes, Mark is a no-nonsense kind of guy who
doesn't waste time getting to the heart of the matter. It almost
seems as though Jesus says all of eleven words to these fishermen (who owned lucrative businesses), and they instantly drop
their livelihood, leave family, and follow Him. More importantly,
though, Mark is communicating something profound about the
invitation to being an apprentice of Jesus. What Mark is communicating is that *being an apprentice of Jesus is central to everything
else in our lives*. It is not a side issue. It is not a peripheral aspect
of life. It cannot be compartmentalized. In fact, it's so pervasive
that it defines who you are.

In the biblical language, the Greek word for disciple is *mathetes*,
which literally means "learner." So what is Jesus doing? He's
inviting Simon, Andrew, James, and John to be *learners of Him*
in such a way that this learning process would be a way of life,
central to everything else. They were learning how to navigate
life in the very ways Jesus did—in the remote details of everyday living, such as, how did Jesus interact in casual conversation?
While hanging out with Peter, James, and John, did He insist on
Himself being the focus of conversation, or did He prove Himself genuinely interested in others through His casual conversations? What sorts of things sparked anger in Jesus, and were they
the same sorts of things that sparked anger in the disciples?

How did Jesus interact with people at a party? As the creator of life, it probably wouldn't be a stretch to say that He brought a whole new level of energy to any party. The disciples also watched the way Jesus engaged those who had differing opinions than He had, and they saw the manner Jesus connected with the disconnected and marginalized. How did Jesus seem to ooze acceptance to these people? The disciples had the luxury of watching how Jesus interacted with people. And this raises several important implications about the way we understand God's will!

First, if being an apprentice of Jesus is the central defining aspect of our lives, then God's will and our process of discerning God's will MUST BE just one aspect of our apprenticeship, rather than the end goal of life. Previously, we were preoccupied with final destinations because finding God's will was the end goal of life. Perhaps there have even been times when we've been immobilized from making a decision due to the fear that God would withdraw His presence from our lives if the decision should go awry. But now we realize that Jesus invites us to be learners of Him; therefore, He couldn't possibly expect a flawless, mistake-free life, could He?

When J.B. Phillips comments on the words of Christ, "Learn of Me," he says, "It still is, as it was originally, a way of living, and in no sense a performance acted for the benefit of the surrounding world. To 'learn' implies growth; implies the making and correcting of mistakes; implies a steady upward progress toward an ideal."[1]

On the other hand, if finding God's will was the end goal of life, then all of life is a performance—an equation to be hacked, a correct proportionate recipe to be mixed, a formula to be deciphered. If God's will is the end goal of life, wouldn't Jesus have said, "Come, follow *My will*," or, "Seek first *My will*"? But that's not what He said. I would think, then, that discerning God's will is consumed in the simple, yet all-encompassing phrase, "Follow Me." And if that's the case, then the central question in life is not, "Have you discerned God's will for your life—vocation, college, spouse, location?" *but*, "Are you becoming a learner of Christ as you navigate life, career, family, dating/marriage, and relationships?"

Maybe right now you're overcome with revolt, saying, "How unrealistic!" Actually, I hope you're not voicing those words aloud. That's just the sort of thing that could create impressions of lunacy in the minds of those around you. Or at least those were my thoughts recently when sitting at a fine local coffee establishment in close proximity to a guy alone at a table staring at his laptop when suddenly he erupted into laughter. Come to think of it, I've almost done this, too, but abruptly caught myself just before an audible sound came from my mouth.

Although I've come up a bit short, I'm trying valiantly to employ humor as a device of persuasion to try to influence you to come over to "my way of thinking" on this. Years ago I read that those who use humor in a job interview are five times more likely to get the job than those whose interview remains solemn and stoic. So I beg of you to be humored here.

Maybe you're not saying, "How unrealistic!" but maybe you're *thinking*, "How unrealistic! Kyle, you're drawing conclusions based on the life of Jesus and His disciples. Jesus' disciples were comprised of several guys whose 'job' was actually just that: to work full-time as an apprentice of Jesus. I, on the other hand, live in the real world and have to make a living by locating a job. A proper amount of currency must find its way into my pocket because there are bills to pay." And I'd say that it's imperative that we remember what sort of "rabbinical school" Jesus was leading. His apprenticeship wasn't confined to a four-walled classroom of teachings aimed at the cerebral cortex. The learning process Jesus was offering had to do with the *art of living*. It was, "Come, let's share life together, and in the living of life, I'll show you the very best way to live." Dallas Willard says it like this, "I am learning from Jesus to live my life as he would live my life if he were I." Make total sense? Willard tries to flesh that out by using his own life as an example:

> My main role in life, for example, is that of a professor
> in what is called a "research" university. As Jesus' ap-
> prentice, then, I constantly have before me the question
> of how he would deal with students and colleagues in
> the specific connections involved in such a role. How
> would he design a course and why? How would he
> compose a test, administer it, and grade it? What would
> his research projects be, and why? How would he teach
> this course or that?[2]

So Jesus' way of apprenticeship didn't compartmentalize life. The context of our various workplaces has to provide one of the greatest training grounds for learning from Him. Of course, the direction of this book isn't intended to explore how that's worked out in the details of the workplace. For our purposes, we'll continue exploring what implications exist about understanding God's will through the eyes of discipleship. But before moving on to our next implication, it's not at all difficult to understand why it's almost unnatural to think of God's will within the framework of discipleship. Nor is it difficult to understand why we typically think that finding God's will—rather than being an apprentice of Jesus—is the end goal of life. It is because in today's Western culture, each of us has had at least a few dozen "rabbis."

OUR RABBIS

Again, at your local dojo, there is no question as to who the sensei is. And in the ancient world, there was no confusion as to who one's rabbi was. The rabbi was the individual out in front of his line of disciples. The disciples had the luxury of watching one individual approach every detail of life. Today, though, we have had dozens of rabbis provide instruction on:

> Morality
> How to relate with our siblings
> How to be a diligent student
> How to handle ourselves in friendships
> What marriage should look like
> How to employ proper table etiquette
> How to choose a vocation
> How to play sports and participate in extracurricular activities
> How to conduct ourselves in business
> How to handle our finances
> And more ...

Realistically, we've had a number of different rabbis play influential roles in shaping how we approach all the various aspects of our lives. Each one of us is a living, breathing patchwork of a number of different people who've left their stamp on us. And like it or not, several of those individuals have vastly different perspectives on what they think is the end goal of life. Our rabbis include parents (foremost), family members, coaches, bosses, career counselors, etc. Willard writes that a couple of the most influential relationships in our lives are our peers and our teachers.

Years ago, I had a particular soccer coach provide detailed instruction on how to take a player down from behind in such a way that could eliminate that player from the game and possibly the rest of his season. Obviously, we'll have various rabbis communicate ways of living that fragment our lives into individual bits and pieces that have nothing to do with the rest of our intended lives.

One of Willard's more profound insights is: "It is one of the major transitions of life to recognize who has taught us, mastered us, and then to evaluate the results in us of their teaching."[3] When we do so, we begin to realize it's no wonder we live with so many inner conflictions. Our lives don't resemble anything coherent at all! One rabbi has instructed us to utilize our God-given talents and gifts to the best of our abilities and work from dusk 'til dawn without lifting our heads, while another encourages us to just let life come as it may and be sure to breathe it all in. One rabbi encourages us to "just pray about it," while another tells us "to get off our duff and do something about it." One rabbi encourages us to live in plenty, while another tells us to live in want. Sometimes these rabbis are Christian, and sometimes not. Sometimes they're two different Christians communicating two very different things. And to make it all easier and simpler to read, some awfully wise rabbis are offering teachings of gold in the most unexpected places at the most unexpected times.

Growing up, my family had a strong sense of community on both sides—my mom's side and my dad's. Most of our extended family lived within an hour of my home town, so we visited extended family at least once every two weeks.

When I was fourteen, we were visiting my mom's side of the family one Saturday afternoon in the middle of summer. This was a typical convergence of about twenty people for Saturday lunch, then football, four-wheelers, and afternoon naps. One

Saturday afternoon, my uncle was teaching me to drive in my granddad's '73 rusted green GMC pickup. This uncle was a very laid-back guy whom everyone in the family absolutely loved. And in this small town, most of the roads weren't nice city streets; most were oil-top roads. So one afternoon, I jumped in the driver's seat of this '73 rusted green pickup with my uncle in the passenger seat. I pulled out of a long gravel driveway, and we started heading down the road. And of course, at age fourteen, it took me all of thirty seconds in this old pickup to get up to fifty miles per hour on a back road where the speed limit was thirty, even though most residents drove at about fifteen.

My uncle turned his head and said in a most nonchalant way, "You in a hurry?" And that's all it took for me to realize, "Oh yeah, we're not even really *going* anywhere!" I was fourteen years old, and it was the middle of the summer. We were just out driving and didn't even have a destination in mind. When we left the house, we never even said, "Let's drive to _____." We just jumped in the truck, and off we went.

Still, it seems there was a little more going on here. My uncle had a greater sense of depth and wisdom, so his question wasn't just directed at maintaining the speed limit and observing the rules of driving safety. It was more than that. This was a sixty-year-old man asking a fourteen-year-old in the middle of puberty an important question in the middle of the summer months when nothing was going on and the fourteen-year-old had no place to be. And it was all in the way the sixty-year-old asked the question. It was *the manner* the question was asked and the way the sixty-year-old carried himself.

My uncle lived his daily life with a distinct sense of presence. He could've just said these very same words in a rapid fire, matter-of-fact sort of way, coupled with a backhand. "YouInA-Hurry?! ... *whack!*" And I would've said "No," slowed down, and called CPS. But the manner he said it seemed to make all the difference in the world. He carried himself with a non-anxious presence that bled into the very way he communicated. And wasn't this the advantage the disciples had? It's not just that the disciples had the opportunity to watch Jesus pray and heal and teach. Specifically, it's that the disciples learned to pray and heal and teach *the way Jesus prayed and healed and taught*. And that seems to make all the difference in the world!

You and I, we hear one person pray, and the manner he prays sounds a bit too grandiose and performance oriented. There's an awful lot of verbage going on that doesn't seem to have a great deal of meaning attached to it. And then we hear another person pray, and he prays in a manner that at least seems more genuine, more authentic, more heartfelt, and more humble. And we think, "Yeah, that's a bit more like it."

We see one person serve, and she serves in such a way that calls attention to her service. Perhaps we don't know what it is, but instinctively something feels backward about her actions. Obviously, she's just acted on behalf of another, so who could argue against that behavior? Until we see another person serve, and she serves others in such a way that doesn't call attention to herself in the process, and we're left saying to ourselves, "Yeah, that's a bit more like it." Unfortunately, I am more often the former rather than the latter.

We see a person in need of comfort, compassion, and sympathy during a difficult time, and one person steps into their world and says all the right things—but something about it seems lost. Another person walks in the door with a gentle, empathetic awareness that seems to communicate beyond mere words to the one in need ... and we're left saying to ourselves, "Yeah, that's a bit more like it." That's a bit more like the life we're called to live as apprentices of Jesus.

This is how discipleship takes place. This is how growth with God takes place. Jesus invites His apprentices to come and share in His life and ministry together, a life that is undoubtedly lived and learned *out there* on the training grounds of the workplace, a class, the hospital, a gym, a club, a restaurant, or a field of play—in essence, behind the steering wheel. Being an apprentice of Jesus is central to everything else, and discerning God's will is just one aspect of our apprenticeship—not the end goal of life!

1. J.B. Phillips, *Your God Is Too Small* (Touchstone Books, New York, NY: 1997) p. 31.
2. Dallas Willard, *The Divine Conspiracy* (HarperCollins Publishers, New York, NY: 1998).
3. *Ibid.*

5

THE PATH OF LEAST RESISTANCE

The metaphor of discipleship reframes the subject of God's will by placing our apprenticeship to Jesus—rather than deciphering God's will—in the center of our lives. Again, if being an apprentice to Jesus is the central defining aspect of our lives, then God's will and the process of discerning God's will is just one aspect of our apprenticeship rather than the end goal of life. And that's just the beginning ...

Typically, when you're trying to draw conclusions about a given subject, the second conclusion could be construed as of lesser value and importance than the first. For our purposes, our first conclusion suggests that being an apprentice of Jesus is the end goal of life rather than "God's will." However, our *number two* should in no way be considered as less than number one. If number one is Michael Jackson, our number two is not Tito. Our number two is also Michael Jackson. No, that's not right. Perhaps this metaphor has already broken down.

Moving on, *number two* is highly important. Be advised of its value. However, it will only make sense when understood through the lens of apprenticeship. It will not make sense if viewed through the lens of Wall Street or Hollywood. So within the framework of discipleship, consider these stories. Stories like the two that follow seem to be fairly indicative of the sort of situations in which the disciples found themselves. In the eighth chapter, the Gospel of Luke says:

> One day he (Jesus) and his disciples got in a boat. "Let's cross the lake," he said. And off they went. It was smooth sailing, and he fell asleep. A terrific storm came up suddenly on the lake. Water poured in, and they were about to capsize. They woke Jesus: "Master, Master, we're going to drown!"
>
> Getting to his feet, he told the wind, "Silence!" and the waves, "Quiet down!" Then he said to his disciples, "Why can't you trust me?" They were in absolute awe, staggered and stammering, "Who is this anyway? He calls out to the winds and sea, and they do what he tells them!" (Luke 8:22-25 The Message)

Now, consider this next story as well. It, too, seems fairly indicative of the sort of life the disciples led (minus the violence— hopefully, the disciples didn't endure beatings of this nature on a daily basis).

> One day, on our way to the place of prayer, a slave girl ran into us. She was a psychic and, with her fortunetelling, made a lot of money for the people who owned her. She started following Paul around, calling everyone's attention to us by yelling out, "These men are working for the Most High God. They're laying out the road of salvation for you!" She did this for a number

of days until Paul, finally fed up with her, turned and commanded the spirit that possessed her, "Out! In the name of Jesus Christ, get out of her!" And it was gone, just like that.

When her owners saw that their lucrative business was suddenly bankrupt, they went after Paul and Silas, roughed them up and dragged them into the market square. Then the police arrested them and pulled them into a court with the accusation, "These men are disturbing the peace—dangerous Jewish agitators subverting our Roman law and order." By this time the crowd had turned into a restless mob out for blood.

The judges went along with the mob, had Paul and Silas's clothes ripped off and ordered a public beating. After beating them black and blue, they threw them into jail, telling the jailkeeper to put them under heavy guard so there would be no chance of escape. He did just that—threw them into the maximum security cell in the jail and clamped leg irons on them (Acts 16:16–24 The Message)

Now, after considering the sort of experiences Jesus' disciples regularly faced, did you notice any similarities? Did you notice any consistent themes? It seems pretty evident that the life of a disciple encountered all sorts of wild adventures, but an apprentice of Jesus in the first century could bank on this: *A life of ease was never promised nor was it expected.* And this raises some serious concerns about the way we understand God's will today, two thousand years later!

Where in the world did we get the idea that God's will for our lives would entail a life of ease and safety? At what point along our journeys did we confuse God for an insurance policy who saves us from ever having to experience times of distress and frustration? Certainly, in the world in which Jesus lived, the early disciples encountered all of the ups and downs of life. Just because they were followers of Jesus didn't mean their lives would be exempt from difficulty. Yes, they were blessed enough to see lepers healed, water turned to wine, and a little bit of food feed more than five thousand. But almost all of them also experienced failure, physical danger, doubt, conflict, and frustration.

Surely, if the disciples ever thought there were stock options or insurance benefits to working for the one true God, those ideas were trashed somewhere along the way. The Gospel narratives in the New Testament reveal that a life lived in close proximity to Jesus is not bland, usual, or ordinary. Quite the contrary. Anyone who chooses this life can expect an amazing adventure—one that involves hazards, risk, and unknowns.

In fact, it seems as though so much of our time, energy, stress, and thought space goes into alleviating "the unknowns." And yet "the unknowns" are inherent to life. Jesus never seemed to give the disciples a heads-up on what to expect. Never does Jesus tell His apprentices, "Alright, once you get to Caesarea, watch out for the wild-eyed lunatic on 3rd Street because he'll be packin' heat and a switchblade," or, "Alright fellas, I'm gonna catch some shut-eye on the ride over. Should a ferocious storm hit with twenty-foot waves, it's not worth waking me up over. We'll be alright." Of course, Luke's account of this storm seems to suggest that Jesus never became anxious or fear-ridden, despite the impending chaos.

So, herein lies a major misconception about God's will—namely, that *God's will is the path of least resistance*. It seems as though the predominant Christian creed that governs our approach to God's will is: If we are truly following God, things will all just pan out ... our road will become much smoother ... and with God on our side, we'll not encounter near as many obstacles in life as other people do.

WHY THE CONFUSION? WHERE'D WE GO WRONG?

Now, in our interactive relationship with God, I do believe that at times God opens some doors and closes others, but our mistake is to confuse an open door for an easy door. And it's not terribly difficult to understand from where this confusion comes. Many of us have truly had experiences when a particular opportunity practically fell in our laps: A job opportunity became available at the perfect location at the perfect time, a newfound relationship sprung up at an unexpected yet much needed time, or a letter of acceptance to a particular school came in the mail at just the right time. And the level of ease at which this opportunity afforded itself might have also sent the wrong message: that because this "open door" swung wide rather easily, the life *beyond* that door would also entail ease and predictability. It's uncanny how often Christians raise a fist at God because a door they thought He guided them through turned out to be full of disappointment, failure, and conflict. I can't help but think that all the while, God was responding, "But I never promised easy. Nor did I promise safety."

Remember, formulas and recipes have to do with predictability and certainty. We plug in the numbers, figures, and ingredients in order to get a specific result, a desired outcome ... a life of 100 percent success, wealth, health, and opportunity ... and in the process, we strip life of any risk, mystery, and adventure. Come to think of it, it doesn't seem as though Jesus ever gave His disciples a blueprint on what they could expect in the journeys that awaited them.

Danielle Shroyer is a pastor living in New Jersey who could

well attest to this mythical understanding of God's will. The story of her life in recent years goes like this:

> In the spring of my junior year of seminary, my husband and I found out that we were pregnant. This was, clearly, not perfect timing. I had a year of school to finish, we were living in a one-bedroom apartment in married housing, and our families and friends were nowhere near us. Not to mention the fact that we were at least three years away from our "target date" for starting a family! We were totally and completely unprepared for parenthood.
>
> I had this "plan" for my life that I felt was at least God-honoring if not God-breathed, but things were not exactly going the way we expected. It was a very strange time for us, one that was both exciting and really scary. And most people did not want us to be honest about that. They quickly sought to calm our fears by saying things like, "God's timing is perfect," or "God's ways are higher than our ways" or, my personal favorite, "God's plan is always the best plan." That felt very shallow, like we were just supposed to blindly accept this major turn of events without so much as a whimper.
>
> Other people gave us Herculean pep talks as if we were Stephen about to be stoned in Jerusalem. They said that God was trying to strengthen our faith, to test us and to refine our hearts. This made me feel like a child gone astray who now had to account for her wandering. And, though a little apprehensive about our new future, I certainly didn't feel oppressed or persecuted, especially not at the hands of God.
>
> We decided to take things day by day, to learn as we go,

and to trust that God would be with us. It definitely wasn't easy. I had to take a considerable load of summer courses and drop some classes in the spring I really wanted to take. We had to convert the dining room of our small apartment into a makeshift nursery. And our families, though able to be here for the birth, did not get to see the daily progression of my pregnancy and of our daughter's early years. It was a bittersweet time.

Looking back over two years later with a second child on the way, I can see God's hand guiding us through that year. Not because I think God made me pregnant before I was ready or because God did this to test our faith, but because I have this extraordinary daughter and because of her I have learned grace and patience and the beauty of unconditional love. And I've learned that despite our best-laid plans, life interrupts, and our task as people of faith is to walk with grace and hope down the road we're given.

There seem to be two basic ways people approach God's will. I used to be the kind of person who sits on the bus and spends the entire trip holding tightly to the map, studying its every mark and symbol. I think God is slowly teaching me to be the kind of person that spends the trip looking out the window and admiring the beauty of the world going by. And I have my daughter to thank for that.

The life of a disciple, "a learner of Christ," has some unmistakably potent direction for us. On a daily basis, we must set before ourselves this question, "Are we becoming a learner of Christ as we navigate whatever this day may hold?" Can you imagine where the state of the Church would be today if those early disciples had aborted mission at first sight of a demoniac, frenzied crowd, storm, or difference of opinion? "That's it! I'm outta here. I didn't sign on for this!"

Thankfully, their expectation level for the types of chaos with which they'd be confronted was different than mine. A couple of years after college, I had a difficult decision to make—difficult because I was content in my current job and making good money. A sufficient amount of currency had found its way into my pocket—and through legal means, mind you. In retrospect, that job has been the only time to this day when I wasn't constantly looking over my shoulder financially. The difficulty about this decision wasn't due to the fact that I had a good job, but because a decision needed to be made about a great opportunity two thousand miles away.

Of course, no real decision would need to be made if the current job I had was lousy, but that wasn't the case. It seems, at times, people underestimate the sheer beauty of pathetic situations. On the road of life, pathetic situations should actually be considered *gold*. Why? Because pathetic situations supply us with indisputable, clearly defined, absolute direction amidst what is usually confusion and fog. And yes, now I've trailed off into utter stupidity.

Consider for a moment, if you will, a current or recent cloudy decision to be made. In the midst of all the confusion and fog, who ever stops to appreciate the pathetic job they had in the past and are no longer wondering whether or not they will pursue? You know without a doubt that amidst the forty-two different options besetting you, there is ONE direction you will DEFINITELY not go. Or, who ever stops to appreciate the fact that though they are having relationship difficulties and trying to discern God's will, *at least* they are not dating the thug they dated four years ago! Or, who ever stops to appreciate the fact that though they don't have a handle on which major to choose, at least they won't be majoring in Poly-Sci—the course they've now taken three times. All I'm saying is that pathetic situations give us bearings. They give us at least an ounce of direction, and even 1 percent of direction is like gold when it comes to decision-making.

But the difficulty here was not that my decision was black and white. Instead, I found myself deciding between what is good and what is *better*—a nice situation in which to be. I was deciding between remaining in my current job of documented success and happy funds or moving many miles away to a potentially better experience—emphasis on the word "potentially." Now, wouldn't decision-making be infinitely easier if the uncertainty factor was eliminated? That one tiny element sure seems to screw things up and wreak havoc on our intestines, but it also seems to be inherent in life. And it definitely rang true in this scenario.

After two months of obsessing over this decision—consulting a variety of trusted individuals and logging hours of prayer and scripture reading—I pulled the trigger and committed to moving two thousand miles away. In the initial month of my new job, the possibilities were endless for this being an excellent experience ... until my primary contact and employer was fired. Uh-oh. Now, not only was my future in this position up in the air, but my previous successful job remained in the rear-view mirror.

Naturally, I did what any devoted and faithful follower of God would do. I hit the panic button, and my mind shifted into overdrive. Immediately, question upon question flooded my mind: "God, maybe I heard You wrong? I was intended to stay in my *previous* job, not this one, right?! Did my lines get mixed up with someone else's? Are You angry with me, and this is the evidence? And now, should I stay in this job or move back and try to retrieve my previous one?" These are all natural questions to ask. In fact, when the rug is swiped out from under you and you find yourself lying on your back, it's inhuman *not* to ask these questions.

But again, in light of the early disciples' experiences, I can't help but imagine God responding with words like, "But I never promised easy. Nor did I promise safety." Though we have intentionally chosen to follow God, that doesn't mean our lives are exempt from disappointment, illness, conflict, and even unexpected tragedy. God's will is not the path of least resistance! And sadly, at times, we are misled into believing that just be- cause an "open door" swung wide rather easily, the road beyond that door will also entail ease and predictability.

And that's not the only reason we've confused an open door for an easy door. There's another reason we typically think follow- ing God will provide the path of least resistance. And this next reason is probably more significant than the first. Certainly, the first plays a role—namely, when a specific opportunity (a job, relationship, scholarship, school, or promotion) practically fell in our laps, it was natural for us to expect that the life that fol- lowed would be easy. But the next reason for this confusion is even more imperative to understand, which is why it deserves its own chapter ...

6

CHAPTER

THE JUNIOR VARSITY
APPRENTICE

An apprentice of Jesus must have an entirely different frame of mind about life and what life will hold. A scripture passage in 1 Corinthians depicts this sort of mindset beautifully. The only question is, can we get into the mind of a first-century Corinthian Christian so as to fully understand what it took to be a Jesus-follower in that day and age? Is this even possible?

Let's start here: The city of Corinth was loaded with sexual perversion, perhaps even more so than what most liberal cities in America have to offer. Perhaps we could begin by deconstructing one of our modern-day forms of sexual perversion—gentlemen's clubs.

Gentlemen's Club. Now there's an interesting term. I'm fairly confident in my familiarity with both words—"gentlemen" and "club." To me, a "gentleman" evokes images of a distinguished, clean-cut man dressed to the nines holding a glass of port in his right hand between two fingers and a thumb and a fine Cohiba cigar fixed between his index and middle finger.

I'm also fairly confident that I understand the word "club." But when coupled with the word "gentlemen," we suddenly find ourselves in an altogether different place that has very little to do with cufflinks, expensive shoes, sophistication, and a dignified address to members of the opposite sex.

Read Mercer Schuchardt wrote a fascinating article in a 2001 issue of *Regeneration Quarterly* on "the cultural victory of Hugh Hefner." One of the many insights he brought to the table was the evolution of the porn industry over the past one hundred and fifty years, and, of course, Hefner's central role in this evolution. In the mid-1800s, "The only pornography available was the really dirty stuff, grainy black-and-white picture cards and stag reels made with old hookers and alcoholic johns. It was a vile business in an underground market. And because you had to physically show up to obtain it, participating in pornography meant publicly admitting that you were a pervert, even if only to a group of other perverts."[1]

Almost single-handedly, Hefner attached a different image to the porn industry. Schuchardt says, "What pornography needed to be profitable on a mass scale was to be removed from the sexual ghetto and brought into the living room ... Thus [Hefner] packaged himself as a Victorian gentleman at the hunting lodge." It's not all that difficult, then, to connect the dots and trace the way the porn industry has morphed over the past one hundred fifty years, from disgusting photographic cards exchanged from one hand to the next in an obscure back alley at 1 a.m. to everyone's living room via the Internet, and, more ironically, to an eight-thousand-square-foot Tuscany-bricked establishment with lush landscaping and a $12,000 brick-stucco sign that reads, "The Gold Club at Preston Oaks."

Ever so subtly, today's culture will slightly modify a few words or phrases in hopes of adding a different context to its current meaning. In the case of pornography, what was at one time a hidden perversion has become a public, visual reality in most cities, and globally in the living rooms of all who own computers. However, to assume this perversion of sex has only happened recently and was without a place in the ancient world would be naïve.

Evidently, there were cities in the first century that make today's most liberal locations look like Mayberry. And for us to even try to imagine a place like Corinth, where sexual perversion, prostitution, and transgendered-sexuality were commonplace, would take quite the imagination. There's no place in America today that is really like Corinth was, where shrines offered to gods and goddesses were featured on most street corners and intersections. So it still takes quite a bit on our part to imagine what this place looked and felt like. In *The New Testament and the People of God*, N. T. Wright says, "It meant that the world view of the entire town was dominated by pagan assumptions, that the visual appearance of the town was dominated by pagan symbolism, that the normal mind set of the average Corinthian was dominated by pagan ideas, pagan hopes, and pagan motivations, and that the normal life style was dominated by pagan practices."[2]

With so many gods and goddesses from which to choose, Corinthians could select any deity to worship. Corinthians believed that a person's overall behavior and morality played little part in whether a god would answer prayers or not. What mattered most in cult worship was observing the rites perfectly in order to receive the approval and favor of a particular god. Cult worship required a cult image of the god or goddess, usually a statue and an altar at which to offer the prayers and sacrifices.

The requests and prayers were presented to the gods as *quid pro quo*; in other words, if the god does what is requested, the worshiper promises to do a specific thing in return. Such a request was absolutely binding upon the worshiper. In tempting the gods to act favorably upon their request, a worshiper might make offerings of food or wine, or the ritual sacrifice and eating of an animal. The sacred meal, then, was the most common ritual practiced by the average Corinthian.

Sacred meals, which occurred as part of certain religious festivals, were special sacrificial banquets given in honor of a certain god (or goddess). It was assumed that the god himself would actually share in the meal; a place was set for him at the table, invitations were issued in his name, and a specific portion of the food served was set aside for the god to enjoy. The ritual of the sacred meal demonstrated the belief that the gods were actively involved in their daily lives and in their communities.

It wasn't that some of the citizens of Corinth went from time-to-time to worship at pagan shrines and temples. The vast majority of them did so. Jewish Christians were definitely in the minority.

But this was the problem for Jewish Christians living in Corinth: Butcher shops served as restaurants, but not only as restaurants—also as idol temples ... which meant that almost all of the meat available in the city of Corinth was probably offered at some shrine or another.

So a few Jewish Christians walked through town looking for a good meal passed by a restaurant/butcher shop/idol temple, saw a particular meat and said, "I'm NOT touching that. That meat was offered up to the goddess Aphrodite." And at times, that's not all they'd see. Sometimes, tensions arose when one of these Jewish Christians walked by this restaurant/butcher shop/idol temple and not only saw this meat, they also saw one of their own Jewish Christians at the table eating to his heart's desire!

Why? One Jewish Christian seeing this meat says, "Nooooo way am I touching that! That's been offered up to the goddess Aphrodite." Another Jewish Christian sitting at the table eating a hearty meal says, "But the goddess Aphrodite *doesn't even exist*! There's only one God, only one Creator. And He made this meat, and this is good" (Genesis 1:31).

In a city like Corinth, every Jewish Christian was faced with this option: Either reject idol meat altogether and become a vegetarian, or eat, eat, eat. But avoiding idol meat conflicted with the strong Jewish belief in the goodness of creation and conflicted with their views about there being one Creator God. If a Jew says, "Oh, I'm not going to eat *that* meat. It's been offered to idols!" that's the same thing as saying, "Idols really do exist!" So, rejecting idol meat conflicted with their belief in the one Creator God.

Or the Jewish Christian could head over to the pagan temple, pay homage to the pagan idols, and eat, eat, eat. But in doing so, lose his/her Jewish identity. Of course, if one did this, they couldn't really call themselves Jewish, for Jews believed in the one Creator God. And paying homage to idols crossed the line.

With these conflicts and this tension in mind, the Scriptures say in 1 Corinthians 8,

> The question keeps coming up regarding meat that has been offered up to an idol: Should you attend meals where such meat is served, or not? ...
>
> Some people say, quite rightly, that idols have no actual existence, that there's nothing to them, that there is

no God other than our one God, that no matter how many of these so-called gods are named and worshiped they still don't add up to anything but a tall story. They say—again, quite rightly—that there is only one God the Father, that everything comes from him, and that he wants us to live for him. Also, they say that there is only one Master—Jesus the Messiah—and that everything is for his sake, including us. Yes. It's true.

In strict logic, then, nothing happened to the meat when it was offered up to an idol. It's just like any other meat ...

We need to be sensitive to the fact that we're not all at the same level of understanding in this. Some of you have spent your entire lives eating 'idol meat,' and are sure that there's something bad in the meat that then becomes something bad inside of you. An imagination and conscience shaped under those conditions isn't going to change overnight.

But fortunately God doesn't grade us on our diet. We're neither commended when we clean our plate nor reprimanded when we just can't stomach it. But God does care when you use your freedom carelessly in a way that leads a Christian still vulnerable to those old associations to be thrown off track.

For instance, say you flaunt your freedom by going to a banquet thrown in honor of idols, where the main course is meat sacrificed to idols. Isn't there great danger if someone still struggling over this issue, someone who looks up to you as knowledgeable and mature, sees you go into that banquet? The danger is that he will become terribly confused—maybe even to the point of getting mixed up himself in what his conscience tells him is wrong ... (1 Corinthians 8:1, 3-12 The Message)

So Jewish Christians living in Corinth (and anywhere else in the ancient world) had a decision to make on a daily basis. Every single day they walked out their door, they were forced to figure out how to stay true to their Christian identity while living in a town like Corinth. In other words, they were forced to figure out how to live in the world without becoming a product of it. Their very lives were defined by this mission and involved much more than just praying at the table before their meals. Their sense of mission went hand-in-hand with their identity as Christ followers—not because they were necessarily leaving Corinth on a mission trip to China, Afghanistan, or India, but just because they were followers of Jesus. Realistically, anyone who strives to be an apprentice of Jesus is defined by this mission—to live in this world but not be of this world—no matter where you live.

And to live in the middle of this tension is the most difficult thing to do, isn't it? Isn't it so much easier to live in either extreme?? It takes very little effort to fully embrace every single thing today's culture throws our way—to be a chameleon, so to speak, where there is zero distinction between us and the world we inhabit. Likewise, it's just as easy to retreat from our culture and alleviate any contact with it to ensure we are not of it. That's just a different breed of chameleons.

"Where do you work?"
"Church."
"Where are you gonna be tonight?"
"Bible study."
"What about tomorrow night?"
"Bible study."

"And the next night?"
"Another Bible study."
"Who are your friends?"
(Counting on fingers) "Christian, Christian, Christian, Christian ..."
"Read anything lately?"
"Yeah, you ever heard of Philippians?"
"What do you watch?"
"TBN."
"Seen the news lately?"
"I don't watch it."

As far as "not being of this world" goes, some are doing as great a job at that as others are doing with "being in this world." But make no mistake, the most difficult thing to do as a disciple of Christ is to live in the smack-dab middle of this tension—to live in this world but not be of this world.

In an article entitled, "Are You In or Out?" Brian McLaren offers a couple of scenarios that illustrate how this works in today's world. In this article, he says:

> I go to a movie. In this movie there are murderers, sex addicts, thieves, and thugs. But even among these desperate and damaged characters, there are moments of tenderness, forgiveness, loyalty, honor, and honesty. As the story unfolds, I look just like everyone else sitting in the theater, eating popcorn and candy, but in my mind I am engaged in a kind of discernment that my movie-watching neighbors are largely oblivious to. Because I have been "set apart" by God's message of truth, I evaluate all I see and hear in the movie by the grid of this understanding. The guy next to me is thinking, 'Nice body on that woman ... cool car ... whoa, neat special effect.' But my mind is humming, comparing the

action and values pictured in the movie with the message of truth I have come to believe.

Or consider this scenario: There's a seedy club downtown in a city near you. Inside the club, there's a lot going on: illicit drugs being sold and purchased and ingested, alcohol being abused, prostitutes soliciting and being solicited, gangs tailing targets and planning violence. Let's zoom in on four people who have just entered the club:

1. Jake is looking for a hooker. He's lonely, desperate, and flushed with cash after succeeding at a robbery in another part of town.
2. Shannelle is looking for a dealer. She's addicted to heroin and badly wants a hit. She was in treatment until yesterday, when she fled the treatment center for the streets. She has no money and is asking herself just what she's willing to do for a hit.
3. Bruce is looking for a chance to show off. He's got a lot of pent-up inferiority and aggression and needs to impress somebody to feel good about himself. Maybe he can start a fight tonight.
4. Donna simply hopes to hook up with someone. It doesn't matter if it's a friend or a stranger. She's just lonely.

Entering the club, stepping over empty bottles and litter, are four others. They look no different from the rest of the crowd milling around on the dirty sidewalk:

1. Marcus is an undercover agent. He's actually looking for Jake, hoping to make an arrest.
2. Charice is Shannelle's sister. She's trying to find her sister and convince her to go back into treatment.
3. Leshawn is an AIDS activist. He's there to distribute

literature to urge people to avoid high-risk behaviors.
4.   Marie is a journalist, writing a story on the band playing on stage.[3]

What distinguishes the second group of people from the first? One word: mission.

In fact, wouldn't we say that this is one of the markers of a spiritually mature person? Spiritually mature individuals have undergone a rite of passage during which their lives have been transformed by a sense of mission. We might even go so far as to say that the steady downward decline of the Church in America exists because many followers of Christ do not see their lives defined by mission. Perhaps the very fact that this word—mission—evokes images of Africa or India and not also New York, Hollywood, Merrill Lynch, Hillcrest Hospital, or Andy Woods Elementary School could be part of the problem. If we take our apprenticeship seriously, then Christians of all sizes, shapes, and colors should see their lives in a different light.

In fact, pastors like me could have unintentionally contributed to this steady downward decline. Of course, I don't think we've ever done this intentionally. The future of our jobs depends on our churches' growth and sustenance. So we would never set out to do damage to our own churches and our own people. Instead, 99 percent of the time, the damage done is inadvertent. It's accidental because it doesn't have anything to do with what we say, but what we don't say. Allow me to try to explain this miscommunication: In high school, seniors can only compete on varsity. Correct? A senior can't play on J.V., and it's usually rare for freshmen to make the varsity squad unless a) they are athletic phenoms or b) they attend a school with a graduating class of four, which forces each freshman to play every sport.

But more often than not, the question confronting every sophomore and junior who play sports in high school is whether
you play on J.V. or varsity. And oh, what a distinction this is!

No matter the city or town, in every high school, a certain
phenomenon takes place among at least a few non-seniors who
find their way onto the varsity squad. Somehow, someway, non-
seniors on varsity have some form or fashion of communicating
to their friends and anyone else in close proximity that they are,
in fact, on the varsity team. In Texas, this phenomenon is a little
easier to spot because a few non-seniors will wear their letter
jackets to school in September when it's still 101 degrees with
a humidity level of 105 percent. At times, though, it's a bit more
difficult to spot. It can be a bit more subtle.

Imagine this: You're a sophomore eating lunch in the cafeteria at
the usual table with your friends. You play soccer. My apologies
here to people who dislike soccer or any football-playing read-
ers who may be offended by this imaginary scenario, but at this
point, the odds of a football playing reader reaching this far into
the book are extremely low. Oh, wow! Now that was uncalled
for. My apologies, again. It seems my apprenticeship with Jesus
has not gotten very far after all. Honestly, I would take a tele-
vised game of the Cowboys and Redskins any day over Real
Madrid and Manchester United. Well, maybe the Cowboys and
Redskins, but not the Redskins and Rams. And I am confident there are, in fact, many football players who enjoy reading
books.

Sorry, so once again, you and five sophomore soccer-play-
ing chums are eating lunch in the cafeteria at your usual table.
"Which lunch am I in?" You are in B Lunch. "Did I pack a
lunch or bring money?" You packed a lunch. "What's in it?"
Enough with the questions, you're bugging me. So, you have

a game today because today is Thursday, the day J.V. always has games. Varsity games are on Fridays; J.V. games are on Thursdays. Everyone knows this.

Among your eight friends at the table, one happens to play on varsity. "Eight? I thought you said five." I did, but you are a very likeable person and have already attracted three more friends to your table in the lunch hour alone. Obviously, you are very popular. The bell rings, all of you get up to head to class, and Mr. Varsity says to all five of you soccer players in a most condescending tone, "Hey, so you guys have a game today?" Now, how could he not know you have a game today? In the annals of school history, J.V. has always played on Thursday. What a jerk!—Several of you almost simultaneously respond, "Yeah." And after a couple of inadvertent fake nasal sniffs, he says, "Well, good luck. Ya'll take it to'em."

Now let's get something straight. *On paper*, that looks like a nice thing to say, correct? But that's NOT what he communicated. Much, much more took place here than meets the eye. These types of scenarios take place on a daily basis ... when on paper, if you transcribed what someone just said word-for-word, you'd think, "Well, that was a nice thing to say!" But that's NOT what was communicated, was it? Girls seem to be a bit more conscientious of this than guys are at times. There are times when my wife and I leave a party and she says, "Can you believe she said that?" And I say, "Said what?" It's almost as if a cryptic, coded language had been spoken, because someone just communicated the very opposite of what his or her literal words actually spoke. And here, although this jerk seemed to communicate encouragement, that is most definitely NOT what he communicated. What he communicated wasn't, "It is my sincerest hope that you guys play lights-out today and beat those guys badly!" Instead, what he communicated was, "Hey *peons*, you J.V. ... me varsity. You are here [hand low]. I am here [hand high]. You—

inferior. Me—superior. You are secondary, less than ... just in case you forgot."

Now, we have already talked about and have established that, as followers of Jesus, every single one of us is called to live in the world without becoming a product of it—in other words, we are all called to be missional Christians. But I have to admit that pastors like me have often put missional Christians going to China, India, and Africa on varsity, and have put teachers, doctors, film students, and social workers on J.V. Now don't get me wrong. We haven't *said* that. But who do we commission? And what callings do we esteem? What callings do we applaud?

The reason the Church has been on such a steady decline is because of this attitude: "Well, I'm not going to China or the Middle East or India, so I guess I'll just be a teacher instead." Or, "Since I'm not going to Afghanistan, I guess I could go to work for Merrill Lynch." (Because, of course we know that money has nothing to do with the kingdom of God, right?—wink wink.)

How about this: What would the face of the Church look like if we began commissioning missional Christians to Andy Woods Elementary School? What would the face of the Church look like if we began commissioning missional Christians to Hillcrest Hospital? Why don't we commission missional Christians to China and India ... and actors living in L.A. and New York? Film students working in Hollywood? Accountants to Phoenix, Dallas, Chicago ...

In truth, as apprentices of Jesus, we must understand that the whole of our lives is defined by mission. And if so, this will radically shape the way we understand God's will. How many of us have, at one time or another, felt as though God was calling us out of a particular work environment precisely because that context wasn't thoroughly Christian? So we opted for a more "Christian" workplace loaded with Christian coworkers and a worldview more akin to our own. From one year to the next, I talk to a number of college students who wind up with roommates of differing worldviews and lacking their own sense of fervent spirituality. Many, then, understand God to be calling them *out* of those relationships and living situations. At times, some will go so far as to say that "they don't have a sense of peace about their roommate."

On the flip side, one of the leaders in our church teaches at a school in a low-income area of town. Her particular school has been guided by solid leadership and a structure that is well on its way to facilitating change among the students. However, she recently expressed to me that the school where she taught might not be the best particular school for her because her level of impact wasn't being maximized. Keep in mind she has a great deal of maturity, but she was considering employment at another school where strong leadership and a healthy structure is not in place. As she began to explain her situation, it became clear that her sense of mission had so defined her role as teacher that it clearly affected her decision-making.

As difficult as it is, all apprentices of Jesus have clearly been called to live out their lives immersed in the world while not becoming a product of it. And the more that sense of mission takes hold of our lives, the better sense of direction we'll have about particular decisions that need to be made.

Some of us, though, are actually employed by Christian institutions, churches, or organizations. So how can this sense of mission be fleshed out when the bulk of our lives happens in a "Christian context"? In my own life, I enjoy playing soccer, so I play on a team comprised mostly of college students in a local men's league. Through this team, I've also connected with a network of local area coaches who coach tons of kids on a competitive level.

Now, I have to admit that this could be the most asinine endeavor that I've ever undertaken. Do you understand how stupid it is for a male of sufficient testosterone, who happens to be a local pastor, to play competitive sports? This is not easy, as my teammates can testify. Perhaps this is the reason one teammate recently introduced me to a new teammate like this: "Hey, this is Kyle. He's the pastor of that church UBC ... [laughing] but it's okay, his halo is a little warped."

And I'm also guessing that sometime within the next four days, I'll no longer be able to physically play soccer. So when my kids get older and can play, I'll probably coach their team and develop new friendships with fellow parents.

Nevertheless, mission is woven into the fabric of who we are as Jesus followers. And this sense of mission should never be separated from the decisions we make—whether they are about a dorm roommate or a college major or a job environment. In light of our mission, then, I'll offer some specific mission-minded questions that we should ask in the midst of any life decisions with which we find ourselves confronted:

> Do you see yourself first as a follower of Christ and second as a teacher, social worker, accountant, engineer, actor, student, doctor, politician, etc., or do you see yourself as an accountant who just happens to be a Christian, an engineer who just happens to be a Christian, an actor who just happens to be a Christian ...?
>
> Do you have a healthy level of expectation as to the trials, resistance, and conflict you'll inevitably encounter as an apprentice of Jesus, or do you expect all of your

decisions to reap a life of agreement, cohesion, and safety? (Note: Some people use this former question as an excuse for distancing themselves as "people of faith" from their non-Christian coworkers or classmates, rather than looking for ways to befriend those with whom they come into contact.)

Do you consider the presence of non-Christians in your sphere of influence—school, work, etc.—a hindrance to God's ultimate plan for your life, or do you understand a world that is thoroughly Christian an impediment to your identity as a follower of Jesus? Does the presence of non-Christians affect whether or not you experience "internal peace" about a given situation—job, school, college major?

1. Read Mercer Schuchardt, "Play Boy! The Cultural Victory of Hugh Hefner," *Regeneration Quarterly*, Fall 2001, p.30-31.
2. N.T. Wright, "One God, One Lord, One People," NTWrightpage. com, *www.northpark.edu/sem/exauditu/papers/wright.html*, accessed August 20, 2003.
3. Brian McLaren, "Are You In or Out?" *Christian Single* magazine, *www. christiansingle.com*, accessed June 12, 2002.

7

CHAPTER

SEVEN MILE BEACH

Main Entry: **par·a·dise**
Pronunciation: 'par-&-"dIs, -"dIz
Function: *noun*
Etymology: Middle English *paradis*, from Old French, from Late Latin *paradisus*, from Greek *paradeisos*, literally, enclosed park, of Iranian origin; akin to Avestan *pairi-daEza-* enclosure; akin to Greek *peri* around and to Greek *teichos* wall

Date: 12th century
1 a : <u>EDEN</u> **2 b :** an intermediate place or state where the righteous departed await resurrection and judgment **c :** <u>HEAVEN</u>
2 : a place or state of bliss, felicity, or delight
- par·a·dis·ial /"par-&-'di-sE-&l, -zE-/ also **par·a·dis·i·cal** *adjective*[1]

Paradise is Grand Cayman. In fact, if I should make the cut in
the afterlife, I will wake up on Seven Mile Beach in Grand Cayman. Jen and I will be reclined on lounge chairs at a 45-degree
angle peering out beyond the white sands into crystal blue
waters.

In heaven, Avery is still four, like she is now. She can't date
and of course doesn't have that little temper she has now. She's
building elaborate sandcastles due to her da Vinci–like artistic
prowess. She's brilliant. I mean, her intelligence is far beyond
the average Central Texas four-year old. It is now, so of course it
would be in the afterlife. Sutton and Jude are two. They've just
eaten, so they still have their little pygmy bellies and are now
on a mission to plow into Avery's ornate creation. Seconds later,
misty white sand flies everywhere, and all five of us—including
Avery—laugh hysterically. Beaming with ear-to-ear smiles on
all five of our faces, we embrace. Then, Jen and I sip once more
from our Piña Coladas and lay back down to the musical sound
of our children's laughter.

The Apostle Paul gave the notion that no one can really relate
what heaven will be like, but Paul never met me. I can describe
it with great detail. I can describe what the skies look like from
one day to the next, the size of the New England Rock Lobster
they feature at every meal, and how many twenty-four-hour
Krispy Kremes are in a five hundred–yard radius.

Unfortunately, though, my image of Grand Cayman isn't without blemish. On a recent trip to the island, I was scuba div-
ing with my wife, father-in-law, and brother-in-law. And first,
you've gotta understand that at the age of eight, I watched the
movie *Jaws* for the first time. Watching it just once was enough
to scar me for life. Today, I can stand in ankle-deep water and
feel like I need a harpoon before I take another step. Honestly,
every time I wade out into more than three feet of water, a jolt

of energy runs up my spine as I start looking for the fin. So you can imagine how calm I am when our guide has driven the boat fifteen minutes from the mainland, strapped a tank on my back, and asked me to "go ahead and step off the back of the boat." Isn't there a stealthier way to slip into the water unannounced? You know good and well that every boat/yacht/catamaran/ship/floating vessel anchored in the ocean has numerous carnivorous sharks that haven't been fed in four weeks circling directly below. So if I'm going to announce my entrance into the deep with a huge splash, our guide might as well bow-tie a fresh blood-dripping carcass to my legs.

Surprisingly, though, I've slowly become a believer in our guide's method of entering the waters. Most dive boats have a platform attached to the back of the boat. When you've got eighty pounds of gear attached to your body, you don't actually feel up for a marathon.

After a wet suit, there's an inflatable vest that has the oxygen tank attached to the back to put on. A couple of hoses run from the tank through the vest, while a couple more dangle (just for looks, I think). Years ago, on my first dive, I accidentally harpooned my dive buddy confusing him for an octopus. Then, of course, there's a mask and a two-foot flipper strapped on each foot.

I've tried sitting on the platform and slowly inching my hind parts along until I eventually tump over and into the water, but the three-foot tank on my back makes this nearly impossible. It also helps having your guide laugh as you try.

His suggestion is altogether different: Stand with both feet parallel on the platform. Take one large step off—large enough so the tank doesn't catch the edge of the platform. Breathe normally through your regulator in Vader-like fashion.

"Continue breathing normally once below the surface of the water" (which seems to be fairly important counsel).

And it never fails. Not one time. The *instant* I'm in the water, I remember why it was so much easier to step off.

Something magical takes place in that split second. In an instant, you leave behind one world and enter another. And these are definitely two very different worlds. In the world above-water, finding a place where you can actually track your thought processes is virtually impossible: a place where there is no jabbering, no freeway noise or interstates, no background music to create a more comfortable atmosphere, no blenders blending or tellers telling, and no refrigerators running or air conditioners cooling or heaters heating. Really, no machines whatsoever. Finding a place above-water where you can hear yourself breathe is virtually impossible. But not below.

Below the surface, that's actually all you hear. When you're sixty feet deep, it's better to breathe slow, deliberate breaths than short, quick breaths. It conserves the oxygen in your tank if you train your entire body to function at a different pace.

This is definitely a different world. There's nothing I'm producing, performing, or exerting on my environment—just absorbing, taking in, breathing deep blues and bright greens. Water is so clear someone looking off the side of the boat could see your every move forty feet below. There are fish of all shapes, sizes, and colors and fish that have created their own shapes and their own colors, moving to rhythms of their own and yet somehow symphonic with the rest of the aquatic world.

There are moments of sheer brilliance. Like on a partly cloudy day, rays of light cut through the water, reaching depths of fifty feet and creating a virtual obstacle course below. Or when you're swimming through a cavern at fifty feet and turn your head, inside the crevice of a rock are two lit eyes staring back without any apparent form or shape—at least as much as you can tell. Or when you're at sixty feet and you've just completely exhaled, your next inhalation hits a brick wall and goes no further. Yes, that's brilliant.

Pause for a moment, if you will, and exhale. No, don't cheat. That last breath of exhale you're holding onto, let that out, too. Now, before you inhale, let's transfer one deep breath of oxygen into inches. Still holding? Let's say one good, deep breath is the equivalent of two feet. Now, if one deep breath is two feet, right now, allow yourself about two inches of inhale and abruptly forbid yourself from taking any more in.

And there we are. At sixty feet, and my dive buddy fifteen yards away. Oh, for a solid breath of air.

I'm thinking this might have been a different experience had I not just fully exhaled.

But no time to lose. On the swim to Scott, I inadvertently gulped a lung-full of water. Twice. It's instinct. When I got to Scott, I grabbed his extra regulator that's also connected to his tank for just these sorts of experiences. Looked up to see how far it was to the surface. Too far. Again, my body instinctively tries to breathe. More water fills the lungs.

In an instant, I feel the immensity of the ocean, and in that same instant, I feel claustrophobic, like I can't escape it. It's consumed me.

In my eyes, Scott sees there's no humor here. With his regulator, I inhale. No air. Only water's coming through. More and more water. I look up again, and for the first time in my life, I genuinely think—with no degree of humor, wit, or sarcasm—this is it. I'm gonna die. No way!

Cuss. It's not supposed to end this way. Like this? This is it?

Cuss. Too young.

This is it.

With his right hand, Scott grabs my vest, and with his left, he turns the regulator right-side up and then does something I couldn't think to do. He taps a button on the flip side of the mouth-piece, clearing it of excess water so I can fully breathe. Never has good clean air tasted so good. By this time, the guide has made his way over to us, and we remain stationary for a few moments while I take in the most meaningful air of my known existence.

Slowly we swim to the surface to regroup for a few minutes. Our guide checks my tank—three-fourths full—then checks the regulator valve and realizes it wasn't opened at capacity. Evidently, before our dive, his coworker checked our tanks, but didn't ensure my valve was fully open to allow the free flow of oxygen. But I'm too strung out to fight. Wisely, our guide, takes us back down to forty feet for another fifteen minutes. He knows if I don't, I'll never dive again. And he was right. Since that day, I've dove numerous times, but not without that experience etched in the back of my mind.

Forever now, my little scuba fiasco has been written on my brain. I never would have thought it possible for a little piece of heaven in the Caribbean to be tainted, but apparently it's possible. Oh, don't get me wrong. I'll get over it. I already have. I've been back since and sat on the back porch of a condo at night overlooking the ocean—not looking but listening to the parade of waves come in and carry my weights out to sea while I sit there in serenity with a satisfying grin plastered on my face. But no matter how often I go back, I still can't rid myself of that little fiasco. My body has already set up an appointment with the travel agent in search of a different paradise, but my instincts tell me I'm missing the point. At times, maybe it's our search for paradise that fuels our search for God's will? And our search for God's will could be fueled by a number of things: a new degree plan or a new house, a new church or a second date, a new school or a new roommate. Merriam-Webster defines paradise as "a place or state of bliss, felicity, or delight," but for different people, paradise may be different things.

For some people, paradise isn't a place like Grand Cayman. For some people, paradise is a person, and at times a very specific person at that. A specific person they dream of marrying. Or maybe that "place or state of bliss" isn't a specific person, but *the idea* of a person who will one day be their spouse. Or perhaps for some people, a living, breathing human being has nothing to do with it. Maybe it's just *the idea of marriage.*

For others, "a place or state of bliss" could be a specific job in a specific building in a specific city. Or maybe it's not the job at all. Maybe it's just the city, the location where various jobs can be pursued. But without a doubt, the priority for living for some is location, not vocation.

Whatever it is, paradise gives us something to shoot for. It gives us a goal, something to aspire to while also supplying meaning for the here and now. But I'm guessing if we stopped the train for a moment and traced the evolution of our goals over the past ten years, we'd find out that there were actually times when our goals weren't just goals. I'll bet there were times when our goals actually became reality, times when we found *exactly* what we were looking for.

I know as I trace my own journey, the experiences that immediately rise to the surface are experiences when my goals and
dreams went unmet, when what I really wanted was just beyond
my fingertips. But if we truly paused to consider what it was
that we wanted ten years ago, seven years ago, and three years
ago, would we always say that our goals were just beyond reach?
Is it possible that was not, in fact, reality? That, in fact, five and
ten years ago, we experienced times when we found *exactly*
what we wanted? We made the team we wanted to make. We
attended the school we wanted to attend. We were given an opportunity to express our talents. It's just that when reality didn't
live up to expectation, our search for paradise picked up and set
its sights elsewhere. And today, we can trace our journeys and
realize this cycle has made the block five, seven, and ten times.

The cycle goes as follows:

> *goal conceived>effort>stress>worry>mint chocolate chip>*
> *effort>stress>effort>stress>massage therapy>goal realized>*
> *relief>time>coffee>new goal conceived>effort>stress>much*
> *effort>worry>stress>worry>sleeplessness>very late night*
> *TV>mint chocolate chip>tired>unload stress overload on*
> *people in close proximity>immediate relief>more stress due*
> *to goals + frayed relationship(s)>mint chocolate chip (glucose*
> *addiction)>effort>worry>stress>effort>much more effort>goal*
> *realized>satisfaction>time>new goal conceived>effort>stress*

Before we can even begin to envision a life in which God
inhabits our decisions, we must first ask ourselves, "Am I fed up
yet with this never-ending cycle, or could I make the block a
few more times before I hit desperation? Or, am I ready for an
altogether different quality of life?

One of the most beautiful mishaps in the history of scripture
interpretation is found in a phrase that's repeated several times

throughout the New Testament. The phrase is "eternal life." It's found in passages such as the hallmark passage John 3:16, "For God so loved the world, that He gave His only begotten Son, that whoever believes in Him should not perish, but have eternal life" (NAS). Naturally, we've always interpreted this phrase as having to do with the afterlife. It's what takes place when our physical bodies are placed six feet under. It has to do with soul immortality. In other words, though we die, our souls aren't stuck with our physical bodies six feet under, but have a non-stop ticket to heaven (of course, a smidgeon of this depends on your views of the afterlife and the all-important debates of whether you are a premillennial dispensationalist or a postmillennial dispensationalist or a supralapsarianist). But actually, the one and only place where "everlasting life" or "eternal life" is defined is found in John 17. In John 17, verse 3, Jesus says, "And this is eternal life, that they may know Thee, the only true God, and Jesus Christ whom Thou hast sent." Oh Mylanta.

So "everlasting life" is not entirely an eternal destiny sort of thing. In fact, it's not even primarily a heaven sort of thing. It's a right now sort of thing! Maybe it would be better to say that "eternal life" has to do with the here and now, but it has eternal implications. Eugene Peterson recognized this when he wrote his contemporary version of the Bible. Listen to the way The Message translates John 3:16: "This is how much God loved the world: He gave his Son, his one and only Son. And this is why: so that no one need be destroyed; by believing in Him, anyone can have *a whole and lasting life*" (emphasis mine).

This definitely sounds as though "eternal life" has to do with more than just the afterlife. With the help of Willard, I'd say that "eternal life" is a life lived in close proximity to Jesus *right now*, in which we get a taste of the sort of freedom and liberation that will be experienced in the afterlife. In other words, "everlasting life" doesn't have to do with where you are (on earth or in heaven); it has to do with the quality of life you inhabit—whether your life is riddled with jealousy, gossip, and envy, or confidence, security, and constructive conversation; whether your life rotates around yourself, or whether you have some sense of an other-orientation; whether your life is preoccupied with future fears and future worries, or whether you can be fully alive and fully present *today*. In his book *Hearing God*, Dallas Willard says, it's "*a different kind of life*," because we've become more aware of the reality of God in and around us, and we're submitting ourselves to it.[2] That's the life of an apprentice of Jesus.

In the year 2000, my wife was pregnant with our first child, Avery, and I can't even begin to tell you how many questions and worries came with that first pregnancy. Questions like, How is this baby developing? Will she come out with an extra amount of appendages, like ears, fingers, or toes? Will she be able to hear? Will she be able to see? What if, right now, she's getting entangled in the umbilical chord, and there's absolutely nothing I can do about it?? Are her lungs developing adequately? What will be the shape of her head? Could it be egg-shaped resembling Adam Sandler, or could it be disproportionately small like Diana Ross?

Does this sound like that of a hypochondriac? Perhaps. But a host of worries seem to consume every inch of dead space in your head until you can't wait until the day of delivery. All of your focus, energy, and attention is set on the due date, because at the very least, all of your questions will be put to rest. It's true. Our newborn might come out with complications after all, but at least you won't have to wonder anymore! Sometimes, it's the constant wondering and the state of limbo that's the real killer, isn't it? You can at least deal with what's in front of your face. It's the in between stages of life that seem to suck you dry.

And amazingly, we got there! We made it to the delivery date, and Avery had the correct number of ears, fingers, and toes, depending of course on how you define "correct." There were some initial scares, but she was released from the hospital after two days with a clean bill of health. I mean, she initially looked like an alien because in the first couple of days, there's no such thing as a cute baby. People come by and say, "Wow, she's soooo cute." And you know they're lying through their teeth, because for the first several hours, her eyes are on the sides of her head, and even you, in all the euphoria, can still see this.

But a weird thing happens. Depending on how delivery goes, all parents go through an interesting metamorphosis within hours or even seconds of delivery. For nine months, a parent will expend somewhere between two thousand and thirty-five hundred hours of worry, guess-work, wondering, stress, dreaming, and doubt, depending on the degree to which hypochondria has set in ... all of which climaxes at the moment of delivery. There—in that moment—all of your questions, dreams, and wonderings have been answered. She has arrived with a fully functioning set of lungs. She can speak, or at least scream. She is not entangled in the umbilical chord.

Ahhhh ... euphoria.

Now, however, you start to wonder *how well* she can breathe. So you frequently wake up at 2 a.m. to walk into her room and place your hand upon her chest to make sure it's still moving up and down, expanding and contracting. Now, you worry about her getting sick, because her immune system isn't fully functioning yet. Now, you wonder if she'll truly be able to see, because a newborn's eyes can't track objects from side to side for eight to ten weeks. And if you can slow down long enough, you'll realize something. You'll realize that, yes, you have left behind all of your pregnancy questions and pregnancy worries.

But you've just traded them in for delivery questions and delivery worries. And the second you're done with delivery, you've just traded delivery questions and delivery worries in with first-year development questions and first-year development worries ... and then second-year development questions and second-year development worries ...

And this is life.

With each "conquered" phase of life comes a new phase of new questions and new worries. For some people, God will grant the insight to see that you have set your sights on the wrong thing, that the point of life is not really the goal or destination, but the journey. New Zealand pastor Mike Riddell puts it this way, "Life is neither the candle nor the wick, but the burning." In other words, life is the in-between stuff, the stuff that takes place between point A and point B.

In her book *With New Eyes*, Margaret Becker writes about a period of time during a sabbatical she took from the monotony of a busy life. She says:

> I've been dormant for quite some time now, derailed by
> the act of living itself. Frozen, encumbered. Gummed
> with goals. Paranoid with purpose. As the morning's
> shades rise, I realize that I've seen only gravel and dirt
> for the last eight years; focusing on the placement of my
> own steps before they struck the ground. I tuned out
> all else. Touch, beauty, and simple pleasures—arrayed
> in constellations—wept as I passed during those days,
> crying to be noticed and valued. I'm sure of it now as I
> close my eyes and attempt to escape the endless reams
> of paper chatter in my mind. I've come to this house
> to right myself in life, to wake up, to rest. I've come to

leave the wheel for a moment and assess my need of it. I've come here because had I refused, I believe I might have blinked and missed another decade.[3]

I think this might have been what Jesus conveyed to Martha. "Martha, touch, beauty, and simple pleasures lie waiting on you every single day crying to be noticed and valued. Life is neither the goal nor the destination, but the journey."

Now, obviously, are goals and to-do lists evil? No way. But they must be accompanied with eyes, hands, hearts, and ears that are attuned to the daily graces of life. It seems as though if Jesus has called us to be disciples of Him (literally in the biblical language, "learners" of Him), then "learning" implies *journey*. Learning implies process, where the spotlight shines not on a particular point or destination, but on the journey itself. This is another reason blueprints, recipes, and formulas are inherently flawed. Blueprints, recipes, and formulas have their eyes fixed on the final product of achievement or a particular point on the map that promises to be the goal of one's existence—where the ultimate fulfillment in life is to be found.

Many, many years ago, Oswald Chambers stated this even more boldly. He said,

> We tend to think that if Jesus Christ compels us to do something and we are obedient to Him, He will lead us to great success. We should never have the thought that our dreams of success are God's purpose for us. In fact, His purpose may be the exact opposite. We have the idea that God is leading us toward a particular end or a desired goal, but He is not. The question of whether or not we arrive at a particular goal is of little importance, and reaching it only comes merely as an episode along

the way. What we see as only the process of reaching a particular end, God sees as the goal itself ... His purpose is the process itself.[4]

May God bless our journeys with Him and give us the awareness to encounter Him in whatever our roads may hold—all things planned *and* unplanned.

1. Merriam-Webster Online Dictionary, *www.m-w.com/dictionary.htm*.

2. Dallas Willard, *Hearing God* (InterVarsity Press, Downers Grove, IL: 1999).

3. Margaret Becker, *With New Eyes* (Harvest House, Eugene, OR: 1998) p. 12.

4. Oswald Chambers, *My Utmost for His Highest* (Dodd, Mead & Company, New York, NY: 1935) p. 210.

PART 3

ALTERNATIVE TWO:

FATHERHOOD

"Life can only be understood backwards; but it must be lived
forwards."
—Søren Kierkegaard, 19th century

8

CHAPTER

UNDERGROUND = COOL

Rather than understanding God's will as a formula, recipe, or blueprint, the metaphor of *discipleship* (or, as we've discussed it, the life of an apprentice to Jesus) helps us reframe the issue in a new way ... or, rather, an ancient way. So keeping this metaphor of an apprentice in mind, we'll now turn our attention to a second alternative—*fatherhood*. And here I should say that, in trying to understand a topic as vast as "God's Will," it will require more than one metaphor like discipleship. In fact, it will require all three alternatives working hand-in-hand to provide a sufficient, thorough understanding

Through the lens of discipleship, we learned what to expect and what not to expect behind "open doors." We also saw how the process of decision-making would be impacted if followers of Jesus took a lifestyle of mission seriously. In fact, not only did the metaphor of discipleship retool our expectations and understanding of a missional life, but it also placed the major emphasis of our lives on *the journey* rather than a particular destination. And as many of us know, from early childhood on, our lives are geared toward placing the full value of our lives in a particular destination rather than in the journey.

But if faced with several options, how do you go about choosing one in such a way that would honor God? No doubt, our desire is to make decisions in life that would have God's stamp of approval, but how can you be certain God is applauding a decision? This is the question to which we'll turn our attention in part three.

Compared to a couple of guys with whom I work, I am musically illiterate. Now, in truth, I don't feel as though I am. Really, I am a lover of the musical arts with a semi-wide variety of CDs including (for the most part) very reputable bands and musicians. A few CDs here and there will go unnamed.

Often I am in the hunt for a new, relatively obscure band— preferably from England or Ireland. Finding such bands fill my wannabe spirit with loads of esteem. I can drive down Franklin Avenue with Avery in the back in her booster seat and my latest CD in the dash and ask, "Avery, ever heard of South?"

"No," she says. And with a satisfactory pumping of the fist motion, I respond, "Yeah! Didn't think so."

It is apparent that my reasons for happening upon newer underground bands are somewhat different from my colleagues' reasons. Perhaps my designation of South as an "underground" band exemplifies my stupidity. Are underground bands "underground" because they are unknown or because they are not yet on a label? I do not know this. I do know, however, that their level of coolness depends on how many people are aware of them. If a large number of people catch on to their creative excellence, then, as it goes, they are no longer cool. Of course, this makes complete sense. But if I happen upon them before they've gone public, then that is yet another one of the many confirmations that I am, in fact, hip. I've always known this— that I am cool. It's just taken a while for those around me to get behind this idea as well.

My colleagues, on the other hand, are not cool. Their reasons for happening upon rising bands are altogether different. They genuinely enjoy listening for musicians and bands that are pushing the bounds of musical and lyrical creativity. They thoroughly enjoy a number of bands, some that even I like as well! Only they know why, and I do not; therefore, their conversation about particular albums lasts a tad bit longer than my typical one-line response: "Errr, he plays that there guitar … good." Or, "Wow, that drummer plays fast-like." Or, "I like the way that moosic sounds to my ears."

In fact, it's usually beneficial for me to catch a description of a particular band in relation to other bands of which I'm already aware. This is usually what we do when trying to describe what we do not know or that for which there is no category. Right? In our efforts to orient ourselves and find our bearings, we compare the more obscure bands with those with which we're more acquainted.

"Have you ever heard Dutton?"

"Well, they're kind of a Coldplay meets Red Hot Chili Peppers." Or, "Well, they're kind of a combination of Jack Johnson meets Weezer with a touch of Jay-Z." What?? And we leave the conversation either disinterested due to the musicians referenced or more curious to hear it for ourselves.

Herein lies the poverty of those of us who are human trying desperately to get our arms around this Being we worship. When trying to describe who God is and what God is like, with what do we compare Him? All we can do is use familiar, human experiences and human analogies, each of which can only paint a slice of all that is God. So we wind up saying things like, "God's relationship to us is like that of a father to his children"—although we know perfectly well that God is not *actually* a physical dad. In all probability, He wouldn't be found on a Saturday afternoon comparing fertilizers at Home Depot or helping little Billy with his homework on Tuesday night. (Okay, sorry. Technically, this is poor theology since God is very much present at any and all of the Home Depot locations and there with Billy, who is working diligently on his studies any night of the week.) We're just saying that although we at times relate God as "father," we also understand that "father" does not fully describe all that is God.

Many people today revolt at the idea of "God as father," because the second we begin speaking of "God as father" in today's broken world, it begs the question: What kind of father are we talking about? Are we talking about a drill sergeant dad who literally rules the house with a heavy hand?—because sadly, that's been a reality for many people in today's world. Many have seen, if not experienced up-close, the physical and emotional damage done to a mother, brother, or sister. That and that alone has been reason enough for some to walk out on church the very instant *"father"* and *"God"* are spoken of synonymously. In truth, families who have no trace of abuse in their lineage are definitely in the minority.

To the reader to whom an abusive father was a reality, my heart goes out to you. I understand the risk I take that this metaphor may not work for you. My invitation: Wade in slowly through part three and see how it goes, or feel free to skip to the next metaphor in part four.

Drill sergeant dads, though, aren't the only form of "father" that comes loaded with baggage when trying to describe God in such terms. We could also be talking about a billionaire business tycoon who is for all intents and purposes absent from the daily happenings of his children. Or, vice versa, perhaps we are talking about a God who is so consumed with his children that He couldn't possibly have any other relationships of significance or interests outside of his family. Naturally, then, his children would be raised with the understanding that the world rotates around them!

WHAT'S IN A NAME?

There's no question a number of difficulties surface once we begin trying to relate God with what we as humans can see visually and touch concretely. That's why at this particular stage in my life, I've come to love the history of our Jewish heritage found in the Old Testament. In Jewish thought, a name is not some random designation of letters. Instead, a name represents the very nature, history, and essence of the thing named. This is why observant Jews avoid writing the name of God. On paper, they will typically write it as "G-d," for fear that the written name might later be defaced, erased, or destroyed by someone who's not accustomed to revering G-d's name in this way.

In my efforts to not box God in, I've come to realize that the very name of our Judeo-Christian God explains exactly who He is. It is a four-letter name represented by the Hebrew letters "Yod-Heh-Vav-Heh (YHVH)," and at first sight immediately tells us that YHVH is *beyond* comparison. In other words, if we were to give YHVH a name like any one of the ancient pagan gods, *we* would be the idiots—for no single name can summarize His nature, essence, and history. In fact, the root of YHVH simply means "to be" and says to us that no name can describe G-d's history because G-d's existence is eternal. The very fact that I reference Him as a "He" proves my inept ability to fully describe YHVH, for G-d is neither masculine nor feminine but at times will showcase both attributes.

There's no doubt the term "father" comes loaded with unwanted baggage in its connection with G-d. That's why one of the more significant rites of passage in anyone's faith journey is when they begin to differentiate their earthly father from their heavenly Father, hanging on to the similarities while discarding the differences. Still, when relating G-d as father in the first century, it was never Jesus' intent to suggest that all of his hearers hold their earthly fathers in mind when trying to imagine G-d. Jesus never said, "Okay, right now, think of your own fathers ... Does everyone have him in mind? Now *that* is exactly who YHVH is!" No. Instead, Jesus told stories that created new realities—not just about how we should respond to YHVH, but about how G-d responds to us as well.

THE UNDIGNIFIED FATHER

On one occasion, Jesus told a story that is typically referred to as "The Return of the Prodigal Son," but it could just as well be known as "The Undignified Father," because it bordered on heresy in the way it painted G-d to those who heard it.

> There was once a man who had two sons. The younger said to his father, "Father, I want right now what's coming to me." So the father divided the property between them. It wasn't long before the younger son packed his bags and left for a distant country. There, undisciplined and dissipated, he wasted everything he had. After he had gone through all of his money, there was a bad famine all through that country and he began to hurt. He signed on with a citizen there who assigned him to his fields to slop the pigs. He was so hungry he would

have eaten the corncobs in the pig slop, but no one would give him any.

That brought him to his senses. He said, "All those farmhands working for my father sit down to three meals a day, and here I am starving to death. I'm going back to my father. I'll say to him, 'Father, I've sinned against God, I've sinned before you; I don't deserve to be called your son. Take me on as a hired hand.'" He got right up and went home to his father.
(Luke 15:11-19 The Message)

I've always been convinced that this realization—this "coming to his senses"—hasn't received as much credit as is due. I know a number of people who have made self-destructive decisions—whether it is in dating, career-choices, or simply the day-to-day managing of friendships—yet have never had the "a-ha" moment of "coming to their senses" and realizing their pattern of behavior as being destructive.

When he was still a long way off, his father saw him. His heart pounding, he ran out, embraced him, and kissed him. The son started his speech: "Father, I've sinned against God, I've sinned before you; I don't deserve to be called your son ever again."

But the father wasn't listening. He was calling to the servants, "Quick. Bring a clean set of clothes and dress him. Put the family ring on his finger and sandals on his feet. Then get a grain-fed heifer and roast it. We're going to feast! We're going to have a wonderful time! My son is here—given up for dead and now alive! Given up for lost and now found!" And they began to have a wonderful time.

All this time his older son was out in the field. When the day's work was done he came in. As he approached the house, he heard the music and dancing. Calling over one of the houseboys, he asked what was going on. He told him, "Your brother came home. Your father has ordered a feast—barbecued beef!—because he has him home safe and sound."

The older brother stalked off in an angry sulk and refused to join in. His father came out and tried to talk to him, but he wouldn't listen. The son said, "Look how many years I've stayed here serving you, never giving you one moment of grief, but have you ever thrown a party for me and my friends? Then this son of yours who has thrown away your money on whores shows up and you go all out with a feast!"

His father said, "Son, you don't understand. You're with me all the time, and everything that is mine is yours— but this is a wonderful time, and we had to celebrate. This brother of yours was dead, and he's alive! He was lost, and he's found!" (Luke 15:20-32 The Message)

Now, in Jesus' day, a man of age did not run. While running proves to be a sign of health in our day and age, it represented something entirely different for older generations in the first century: disgrace. Therefore, it is one thing for Jesus to tell a random story like this involving a wayward son, a jealous brother, and a disgraceful dad, but the story becomes even more explosive when told to certain crowds who knew *exactly* what Jesus was suggesting!

The prodigal son stands for the people of God. The older son represents Israel. And in a day and age that esteemed YHVH with fearful reverence, the undignified father represents ... G-d?? Are you kidding me? In retelling Jesus' story, the spotlight's focus has always centered on the prodigal son, but this profound story operates on so many levels at once that it becomes difficult for us to fully appreciate its depth!

When the prodigal son asked for his share of the inheritance, his act could just as well be interpreted as wishing his father dead. An inheritance or estate was something assumed at the time of a father's death, so this act alone is a slap in the face. And how does the father respond? When the son essentially rejects his relationship and future with his father, we see the father accommodate his son's request. In fact, do you think the father had a fairly good feel for what would happen to his money and the road that lay ahead of his son? I do. I think, in all probability, the father knew *exactly* what sort of lifestyle the son would choose. In other words, parents are fully aware that there is a specific *kind* of parenting at work here. And this kind of parenting doesn't have to do with Stalin or Mussolini, because God doesn't function as a dictator, but as one who guides. That is, children, by and large, live with their parents' guidance, but not their domination.

There is a progression that takes place among parents in their relationship with their kids. Parents have an overarching concern not just that their kids will make good decisions in life, but more so that their kids will develop and mature in the process. That's why there are many times in life when parents will see their child heading down a dead-end road, but the parents won't always intervene! Why? Because the parents are psychotic and secretly want their child to fail? No. Because the parents are allowing their son or daughter to find out for him/herself that that road is, in fact, a dead-end road and hopefully mature in the process. I think, in the same way, this father in the story probably knew the direction his son would be headed, but he had to allow his son to experience the dead-end himself.

So what does the metaphor of fatherhood have to say to us about understanding God's will? Well, initially it helps us reframe this issue of God's will from God's perspective rather than from ours; and often, God's primary concerns aren't our primary concerns. In fact, herein lies another myth about God's will—namely, that God's will revolves around *what you do*. And the reason that is a myth is because God's primary will does not revolve around what you do, but *who you are* and *who you are becoming*. Once again, our approach to God's will is rooted in our perception of who God is in the first place. And just as we previously saw that the god of 100 percent does not exist, we see "god as dictator" does not either!

BUT THE DECISION IS HIS WILL

As we unpack this fatherhood metaphor, McLaren provides an excellent scenario that gives us handles on how we might now approach God's will. He writes,

> I have four kids, including a son in college. He is a good young man. Imagine he calls me on the phone and says, "Dad, what is your will for my major in college?"
>
> I would say, "Son, I have raised you to this point in your life so that you can make that decision."
>
> "Yes, Dad," he replies, "but I want to do your will, not my own will. So, please tell me what major to choose."
>
> "Son," I'll say, "I'd be glad to help you think this through. For example, we can talk about how much

you hate history and calculus, and how much you love writing and business. I think I can help you eliminate some options, but I really want you to decide this."

"Dad, don't you love me? What if I make a mistake? I just want to do your will!" he says.

"But, Son," I'll reply, "it is my will for you to make this decision. Again, I'm glad to talk with you and help you think it through. But my will is for you to grow up, be a man, and make a life for yourself by making decisions, hard decisions, like this one. And believe me, whatever happens, whether you major in business or art or physics, whether it goes well or not, I will be with you. You can count on that, no matter what." The point is that he lives with my guidance, but not my domination, because he's my son, not my lawn mower.[1]

In other words, within the context of Brian's relationship with his son, his will is precisely for his son to make this decision! I vividly remember reading this illustration for the very first time years ago and leaving the page with my shoulders, arms, and legs feeling noticeably lighter. It seems as though there are countless people poised and ready to respond to decisions you make, saying, "I know that's what you want to do, but what does GOD want you to do?" As if anything you want couldn't possibly be what God wants, too. And that then becomes the protocol for understanding what God wants to see happen in a particular situation: Whatever you want, do the exact opposite, and you'll be right in the middle of God's will.

But what if my desires are God's desires precisely *because* they're my desires? Make sense? In other words, what if the longer I purposefully strive for a life inhabited by God, the more my desires connect up with God's ... because it's just a natural process that takes place day-by-day, month-by-month, and year-by-year as I'm learning more and more what sort of life pleases God.

One of the reasons I find this father/son illustration so helpful is because it indicates that there is a history of relationship involved here between the father and his son. These aren't two random individuals who have nothing invested in this relationship. It's a father and a son who evidently have a strong relationship in which the father has played a vital role in the son's development, and the son has come to a place of valuing his father's opinions and advice.

Likewise, people who have a history of relationship with God, in which they've come to a place of valuing the things God values, will hopefully be more prone to making sound decisions because they already value prayer, scripture reading, the use of their God-fashioned brain, and the input of those in their community of faith. Obviously, prayer, scripture reading, and our communities of faith play vital roles in refining our sense of direction, but in the end, we must own our decisions without pawning them off on God or others, or we will never take responsibility for our lives and experience the growth and maturity found in the process of decision-making itself.

Keep in mind, though, in suggesting it is God's will for you to make this decision, are we advocating blind, Lone Ranger, heat-of-the-moment decision-making? Of course not. Again, *within the context of relationship with God*, God's will is often actually for us to make the decisions, even difficult decisions in life. And why would God want such a thing? Because it's in the process of making difficult decisions in life that our faith journeys seem to accelerate! It's in the decision-making process itself that we learn to take responsibility for ourselves and experience the growth and maturity that's in store. Can you see how the metaphor of fatherhood also resonates with the metaphor of discipleship (or apprenticeship)? Whether you're talking about discipleship or fatherhood, the primary goal of our lives is centered in becoming a whole-life learner of Christ.

Certainly, we can be more precise here in defining exactly what we are talking about when suggesting something as unusual as "God's desire is for **you** to make this decision." Are we trying to promote a lifestyle of isolated individualism or decisions made in the emotion of the moment? Absolutely not! Let's say you and I are having coffee one day while you explain a specific decision to me that you are mulling over and a direction you were leaning. Without an idea as to who you are and what your history entailed, at some point in the conversation I specifically ask: "What do your friends and family think of this decision? What do those who have a vested interest in your well-being think?" Obviously then, if nine out of ten of those individuals are adamantly voting in the opposite direction of where you are headed, I'd strongly encourage you to reconsider. This is another reason I love the metaphor of fatherhood, because fatherhood presupposes that we exist in a family. And a family is a context of relationships in which we live, are shaped, and make choices. And as followers of Christ, our "family" includes many more people than those in our immediate family. As a member of this family, it's important to recognize that we are not the only child. Just as others help guide and affect the decisions we make, our decisions also affect them.

Also, just as we're not advocating Lone Ranger decision-making, we're also not encouraging emotionally driven, impulsive decision-making. For instance, I wonder how many dating couples have committed the rest of their known lives to one another after two months of blissful dating or without having ever undergone a single argument or conflict? Or, how many people have committed their futures to living in a foreign country at the end of an intensely emotional religious service?

Instead, there's a reason God created us with a brain. Our brains, if listened to, can do an excellent job of combating impulsive decision-making.

For example, I'd never encourage a dating couple to pull the trigger on marriage if both individuals are completely oblivious to their own personal "issues," their destructive tendencies that can lead to the relationship's ultimate demise. And I'd never encourage someone to commit his or her future to living in a foreign country without the experience of actually spending significant time there or truly knowing how adaptable one really is.

Honestly, I hate to admit this, but there was a time when I used to equate God's direction *only* with opportunities that made no logical sense whatsoever. Years ago I had a fascination with the absurd. Common sense decisions were too bland and easy. But the absurd—the ridiculous—these could only be the promptings of God's hand because they demanded an unheard of amount of faith.

If I were to trace the origins of this ridiculous fascination, I'd be prone to think much of it is rooted in our culture's rejection of anything ordinary. Anyone who spends much time watching commercials will quickly see the continual excitement, drama, and absurdity that's promoted on behalf of a particular product—shampoo, soda, etc.

As a freshman in college, I was asked to have lunch one day with a guy I had known just two weeks. And although we had actually talked a total of four times, he spewed enough kindness to last me six years. This should've been my first red flag. It's the sort of thing cults are made of: Immediately intoxicate them with one personal compliment after another, and they'll lose control over their intellects. Within seconds, they'll be won over to your side, believe what you want them to believe, and buy into whatever you want them to buy into.

The first few minutes of the lunch, he explained five to seven reasons why *I* was the guy with whom he wanted to propose this business opportunity—what set *me* apart from "the average guy." Of course, it only took two or three compliments before I was thinking to myself, "Wow, now this guy is *really* cool. I could see us becoming really good friends." I mean, he seemed to like me as much as I liked me, and that's got all the makings of a good friendship.

Soon thereafter, he opened a professionally-designed folder on the table in front of the two of us and began to explain "the opportunity of a lifetime." Over the next thirty minutes, I was inundated with figures—how much I could make within three months, six months, a year, two years ... The possibilities were endless! In the first fifteen minutes, I found out I could make a six-figure salary by the time I was a junior in college. All I had to do was invest $750 up front and begin building a "network of investors" who would pull in other investors, and so on and so forth. This is just the sort of opportunity that (to me at the time) seemed to have some key characteristics of divine influence:

- a sudden change of direction from out of the blue,
- dramatic flair,
- extreme risk, and
- guaranteed overnight transformation.

Hmmm. God may be a God of miracles, but should I bank my future on them?

You've gotta appreciate the beauty of this. I knew next to nothing about this guy, and within forty-five minutes, I was overloaded with a dizzying array of potential salaries "that could be *mine*." And then, after I was asked to digest this load of information, he informed me that I "needed to decide quickly because the window was closing." He didn't know how long it would be before the entry level fee of $750 would double.

Thankfully, though, when I began putting pen to paper, I remembered that I didn't have that much in my checking account! He started pressing the issue, and my instincts and intellect finally woke up. In retrospect, I can see that my fascination with the absurd was rooted in self-destructive and unhealthy behaviors. Today, I've come to realize that any opportunity (financial undertaking, relocation, career change, ministry opportunity) that presents itself in an emotionally-hyped context requires even greater amounts of discernment. All in all, emotion *has to be* one of the more beautiful creations of God, but if left unchecked, it can also become the most dangerous.

1. Brian McLaren "Across the Great Decide," *Christian Single* magazine, *www. christiansingle.com*, accessed June 12, 2002.

9

CHAPTER

OBEDIENCE SCHOOL
AND PLAYING GOD

The Scriptures say, "Children, obey your parents in the Lord, for this is right. 'Honor your father and mother'—this is the first commandment with a promise: 'so that it may be well with you and you may live long on the earth'" (Ephesians 6:1-3 NRSV). Of course, the ambiguity that all children and parents must figure out is, at what age is a child no longer a child, and at what point do parents slow down parenting?

My family went by the modified version, "As long as you're living under *my* roof ..." When I was in high school, our rules were distinguished from the rules in college when I was home for the summers ... and come to think of it, when I was home *after* college.

I remember one of the first run–ins with my parents during this gray, transitional time took place the first summer after my freshman year. I walked in the door the first Friday night of the summer at 2 a.m., and the house alarm sounded off a half-second beep. At the time, it didn't sound short. To me, the alarm sounded like a "cute" little two-year-old who's just been given a toy battery-powered cell phone and thinks it's a piano. It sounded off for what seemed to be eight minutes—I think playing Tchaikovsky.

My parents intentionally set up the system to signal any time a door or window of the house was opened, precisely for this reason. Instantly, they'd know when I or another sibling had gotten home. That night, I had meant to rig the alarm before going out, but it seems I forgot.

Evidently, my assumptions about the college curfew were slightly off the mark. I was thinking it would fall approximately at dawn, and if that was the case, then I had gotten home well before curfew. In fact, 2 a.m. meant I was the good kid who didn't care to maximize the allotted time, but instead, had gotten home to spend quality time with the parents. Apparently though, I was mistaken, and the learning curve took a hard, unexpected turn.

For our family, the time when children stopped being children came closer to the time when the kids graduated from college. Although trying to decipher the *point* at which children stop being children and parents slow down parenting can be really difficult. Is it actually a *point*? Is it a specific day and time? Is it high school graduation after you've walked the stage, or college graduation? Most likely, it's a process, not a single day—a process that actually begins early in a child's life when parents give their kids room to take responsibility for their own lives, bit by bit. And this process takes place not only on behalf of the children who are learning to stand on their own two feet, but also on behalf of the parents who are confronted with the mind-boggling feat of letting go. So when the Scriptures encourage children to obey their parents, we have to ask at what point children stop being children. In other words, we're making the assumption that it's probably not a good thing for a forty-year-old to be living at home with his/her parents.

But what about children of God? In relation to God, are we not always children? I mean, at what point do we cease being children of God? Never, correct? Who could ever get to a point at which they're no longer reliant on God? Or, who could ever say, "I've come to a time in my life when I've stopped 'obeying my heavenly parent' and looking to Him for direction." No, we must always obey our "heavenly parent" and look to Him. But I wonder if it's possible to have a forty-year-old still living at home, "spiritually speaking."

Here's what I mean: Try doing a word search for the amount of times "obey" or "obedient" comes up in the Scriptures. The results are ridiculous! Before even getting to the New Testament, the list is several pages long. One of the Old Testament prophets spoke, "To the Lord our God belong compassion and forgiveness, for we have rebelled against Him; nor have we *obeyed* the voice of the Lord our God, to walk in His teachings which He set before us through His servants the prophets" (Daniel 9:9-10 NAS, emphasis mine). Or, in the New Testament, the author of Hebrews wrote, "And having been made perfect, He became to all those who *obey* Him the source of eternal salvation ..." (Hebrews 5:9 NAS, emphasis mine). This word "obey" has some extraordinary potency, or the various writers in scripture wouldn't have used it so often. Of course the ancient authors didn't actually use our word "obey." They used one of the Hebrew words like "abah" or a Greek word like "hupakoe." And even still, I dig our English word "obey" for one reason in particular—because, at times, there could not be a more fitting word to describe what it's like to follow God in today's feeling-driven society.

Think about it. When you hear the word "obey," there's never even a tinge of emotional consideration attached to it. It's like, you know how God has called us to live lives free of gossip and slander, envy and bitterness, deceit and self-indulgence? But often, it's almost as though we can't help ourselves? For me, at times, it comes down to whatever mood or current emotional state I'm in. I live the kind of life I *feel* like living that particular day or that particular hour, and I end up doing the very things that damage myself and those around me—purely because that's how I *felt* at that particular time.

Well, "obey" suggests that there are times in our daily lives when we must simply deny our feelings and instead be governed by our will. And the strength of our will dictates how often we can refuse our emotional impulses. That's why I dig this word "obey" so much, even though I have difficulty fleshing it out. And perhaps that helps define "obey" and provides the reason so many of the biblical writers came back to this word time and time again.

I have to admit, though, that I've also carried a bit of baggage with this word "obey." For instance, when the Old or New Testament writers encourage their audience to be obedient, how should we understand "obedience" in relation to God? Should we be thinking "obedience" in terms of a dog and his master? Like, dogs have "obedience schools" where they learn tricks, commands, and appropriate bathroom locations. So, is Scout's obedience school the best mental image to relate the sort of "obedience" we're trying to pursue as God's children? In other words, if God created humans as the pinnacle of His creation, why would He then relate to them in inhumane ways? Why would He order His little pawn pieces around as though they were nonhuman, rather than allow them to express who they are intellectually, relationally, and creatively?

And if, in fact, God's will is for us to make decisions on choices with which we're confronted, then what do we make of the oft-used phrase, "The Lord told me to ..."? This phrase seems to be on the résumé of any Christian who's spent considerable time in the Church. Personally, I'd love to be able to say these words never once played a part in past break-ups, but it would be in my best interest not to say such a thing for fear a storm could quickly begin brewing overhead.

The reality is, "The Lord told me to ..." is a commonplace phrase that can be heard within the Christian community, whether the conversation is about ditching a relationship or starting a band. However, in recent years, hearing such words from a preacher on TV or a college student who's dropping out to move to Europe hasn't made me more enthused or assured of the direction they're headed. Instead, I've been left with a tinge of apprehension over whose convincing who. Had God convinced them of the direction He wanted them to go, or had they tried to convince God of the direction they were headed?

Perhaps, now, within the framework of *fatherhood*, our goals have shifted. Previously, we wanted the certainty of being able to say, "Yes, God has decisively spoken. He has handed down His verdict. His exact will is undoubtedly for me to ..." But now, we understand that 100 percent certainty is simply one of the many luxuries we as humans have not been afforded. Wouldn't it be safe to say that there is only one living being who knows *all*? And we as humans were simply not created with that ability. The Apostle Paul alluded to this fact when saying, "For now we see in a mirror, dimly, but then we will see face to face. Now I know only *in part*; then I will know fully, even as I have been fully known" (1 Corinthians 13:12 NRSV, emphasis mine). In fact, what if *certainty* has never been part of God's desire for our lives? Because 100 percent certainty with anything in life—finances, job security, illness, the future—would create the illusion that we don't really need God after all.

cer·tain·ty *n. pl.* **cer·tain·ties**
1. The fact, quality, or state of being certain: *the certainty of death.*
2. Something that is clearly established or assured: "On the field of battle there are no certainties" (Tom Clancy). Certainty implies a thorough consideration of evidence: "the emphasis of a certainty that is not impaired by any shade of doubt" (Mark Twain). Certitude is based more on personal belief than on objective facts: "Certitude is not the test of certainty" (Oliver Wendell Holmes, Jr.) Conviction arises from the vanquishing of doubt: "His religion ... was sub stantial and concrete, made up of good, hard convictions and opinions. (Willa Cather).[1]

Earlier in part three, McLaren offered a father-son scenario that helps describe the role he desires to play with his own son. The son, eagerly desiring the will of his father, repeatedly asked for direction. But what if other desires are at play beneath the surface as well? What if the son's desire for his father's direction was at work AND the son's desire for certainty?

Think of it this way: When God found such delight in creating man and woman (Genesis 1:31), it wasn't because He had just created angels, gods, or demigods. No, it was because He took great satisfaction in creating *humans*—living people who have an amazing capacity to love, share, relate, grieve, laugh, cry, move, smell, taste, create ... but people who also share some destructive potential as well. And according to our story in Genesis, the most disastrous experiences that take place in this life happen when humans strive to dethrone God by *being Him*. In Genesis, it was the desire to be God that led to the Fall. In fact, it's this deep-seeded desire to be our own god that has always provided the launching pad for our destructive behaviors and sinfulness.

If you're even half as corrupted as I am, then you, too, are usually in a place of wanting more power than you have, more control than your coverage extends, and more knowledge than you have access to. For example, we all share this deep sense that so much of our lives can't be neatly boxed up and bow-tied. So much of our lives isn't as tidy as we want it to be. And when we can't seem to control every aspect, we respond by micromanaging as much of our lives as we can. When that doesn't satisfy our needs, we micromanage the lives of those around us as well. All that to say, what if our desire *to know* and *to speak as though we know with certainty* is just another one of the many ways we try to reject our humanness in all of its limitations and be God?

Let's suppose there are two couples. The first couple has been dating two months, while the second couple has been dating long enough to have experienced some ups and downs. The second couple is at a place in their lives where marriage is a healthy, exciting, and realistic next step. Now, feel the difference for yourself between a statement made by the first couple and a statement made by the second:

Couple 1: "The Lord told me to marry Jennifer."
Couple 2: "Jennifer and I are definitely exploring the possibility of marriage, because we're taking our relationship seriously, and we seem to have the makings of a good marriage: God's involvement, genuine love, compatibility, and more."

Couple 2 may even go on to say things like, "Our relationship isn't governed by constant strife, and those who know us well have been fully supportive of our relationship."

With the metaphor of fatherhood in mind, can you feel the difference between Couple 1 and Couple 2? At face value, Couple 2 sounds like a couple who've weighed in on the seriousness of this decision and gone through the proper channels (prayer, scripture reading, the advice of their faith community, reason, and perhaps an intuitive sense of peace). They sound like a couple who are deeply aware of the vast distinction between God and themselves—that God is God and they are human—it even feels as though there is a sense of humility to Couple 2. And they also sound like a couple who are taking responsibility for their decision. Again, there is something profoundly mature about owning the decisions we make and owning the decisions we've made in our past.

RULING OUT INTUITION?

So in our efforts to not play God, does that rule out instances of acting on intuition? Not at all! But, in the end, whether our direction is based on intuition or pure logic, we should always accept those decisions as our own.

Intuition is one of the more fascinating aspects of our God-fashioned lives. It echoes one of the fundamental threads woven into the fabric of our created world—namely, that there *is* a way of knowing that happens at times without the use of logical thought processes. In the seventeenth century, Blaise Pascal said it this way, "The heart has its reasons which reason knows not of." (Blaise Pascal, *Pensees*)

As humans, we even have this *sense* that things are not as they should be ... that we are not living life as it was meant to be lived. And there is something within us that always impedes our efforts in living "the good life." Sure, part of this knowing is logical. But part is not. Part of this knowing is a *sense*, a perception. And this sense is just as much a part of our human selves as reason or emotion, although it can't be measured and isn't visible, concrete, or tangible.

Intuition echoes mystery. It points to a world where matters of faith and life can't always be reduced, especially not into formulas. In fact, in a world where intuition exists, theology doesn't have to fit together like a jig-saw puzzle. Mystery is embraced, not shunned. Paradox resides. And humans are reassured that they are, in fact, human and not God—that they do not know *all*. In the end, intuition reinforces our place in this world ... that *we are not God*. We are most definitely *human*.

I've definitely made decisions in the past based on intuition or "what my instincts were telling me." Some of those decisions turned out beautifully, and some did not. Certainly, the use of intuition is not fail-safe. In fact, there are *some* decisions in life that should never be made on intuition alone—marriage, college major, and a change of career are a few. Duh. And still, let's be clear ... whether we are moving on our own sense of intuition or another form of direction, the metaphor of fatherhood reminds us to take responsibility for *every* decision made.

1. *The American Heritage Dictionary of the English Language*, 4th Ed., (Houghton Mifflin Company: 2000).

10

CHAPTER

CODEPENDENCY

co-de·pen·dent or **co·de·pen·dent** *adj.*
1.   Mutually dependent.
2.   Of or relating to a relationship in
       which one person is psychologically
       dependent in an unhealthy way on
       someone who is addicted to a drug or
       self-destructive behavior, such as
       chronic gambling.

n. One who is co-dependent or in a co-dependent relationship.

co'de·pen'dence or **co'de·pen'den·cy** *n.*[1]

Several years ago, I read a theory that I wasn't aware some atheists and agnostics held. At first reading, I found the theory ludicrous and thought it to be a lame accusation, but the more I've thought about it, the more I've thought there's actually a bit more merit to this theory than I originally believed. J.B. Phillips summarized this theory in *Your God Is Too Small*, saying that all religion is "an attempt to return to the dependence of child-hood by clinging to the idea of a parent."[2] I would say they are alluding to a term commonly tossed around in psychology called "codependence."

Initially, after I first heard this, I got defensive and said to myself, "But Jesus Himself said that those who play a role in the king-dom of God must 'become like little children'" (Matthew 18:3). So surely there is an aspect of our faith in which it is good to be childlike, right? Absolutely. A few years ago, I remember try-ing to get some work done over lunch at a local restaurant. The booth in which I sat was located along the aisle two tables away from the entrance to the restrooms. With my back to the rest of the restaurant, I sat facing a wall on which hung a beautiful van Gogh print. Of course, I would've never caught sight of this work had a kid approximately six years old not been heading to the restroom when the painting grabbed his eye. Some-thing about it stopped him dead in his tracks directly beside my booth. Instinctively, he propped himself up on my table by his elbow without batting an eye, and no joke, he stood there motionless, staring at the wall for at least thirty seconds with his elbow inches away from my opened notebook. After thirty seconds or so, his feet were evidently forced back to the ground because he abruptly turned his head in my direction for a split second. And I just said, "Cool picture, huh?" And without a word, on he went to the restroom.

Clearly, he could sense the momentary awkwardness in the realization that this table he was leaning against wasn't occupied by his parents. Of course, I didn't care. But I did care that this annoying six-year-old broke into my world and destroyed the rhythm of my life for at least a couple of weeks. I couldn't get this experience out of my head. And dangitt, there it goes again! What is this?? Right now I'm sitting in a café one table removed from a family of four. A pudgy little girl no more than five or six has gotten up from her table to twirl like a ballerina, and *now she's twirled on over right beside my table.* What is this?? It's the cutest flippin' thing I've seen all day! (or at least since I left the house a couple of hours ago). This little five-year-old can pirouette like the best of 'em!

What is it with kids? No matter where they are or when they're there, they have this sacred ability to be *fully present.* Physically, mentally, emotionally, and soulfully *there.* That is, wherever they are, they are *there*—and nowhere else. Unlike me. I can be pushing my boys on a swing in the backyard, but be mentally absent, problem-solving issues at work. I'm pretty far from mastering the sacred art of presence. So in this respect, childlikeness is worth embracing because it taps into the core of how we've been created by God—to be fully present, fully alive.

However, maybe there are aspects of childlikeness that are not worth embracing. Maybe there are other aspects of childlikeness that are worth growing out of? In fact, at the moment, I'm wondering if there's a difference between being child*like* and child*ish?* The Apostle Paul seemed to say something of the sort when he wrote, "When I was a child, I spoke like a child, I thought like a child, I reasoned like a child; when I became an adult, I put an end to childish ways" (1 Corinthians 13:11 NRSV).

On at least one occasion, Jesus encouraged those who wanted to participate in the kingdom of God to "become like little children." He spoke these words in the midst of a debate over which disciple was the greatest and in a culture that placed women and children at the bottom of the social totem pole. In other words, Jesus was encouraging His followers to be childlike in holding little regard for status, titles, and position. He wasn't encouraging His followers to live the life of irresponsibility, reckless concern, and codependency.

When my twin boys were born, Avery was almost two. Jen and I knew well before the boys were born that once they entered this world, our mission as agents of God would be to protect our baby boys from the hands/weapons of their sister. We've known this about our little girl for a long time. She is not for the faint of heart and is not as I've seen other little girls be. I've seen other little girls her age sit primly and quietly at public restaurants. Evidently, they have been raised differently. Jen and I, though, scratch our heads and wonder what went wrong as we drop an extra five dollars tip for nuking that little five square feet of space.

There have been countless adults who've met my little girl and said, "Now isn't she just the sweetest thing!" And I think this is part of her strategy. Avery would be deathly similar to the Venus Fly Trap. The Venus Fly Trap is the femme fatale of the plant world. She lures large insects by her extraordinary color, taste, and scent, and just when the insect is within her grasp, she snaps close and squeezes her victim to death within seconds.

Of course, I would say that Avery is awfully cute, but what some people don't know is that her cuteness is her allure. Just when she has lulled you to sleep with illusions of peace and safety, she strikes with brute force. And this is not the force and power of a toddler. Well beyond. When we're in conversation with other young parents and they've just described the yellow stuffed Care Bear their little girl is "so into," how do you respond and say, "Oh yes, I know what you mean. Avery is into ... um, how do I describe it? What's the word for it? ... *Violence."*

So Jen and I knew well ahead of the game that the twins would be prime targets—small, defenseless, and weak. Often, we tried to model the word "gentle" so she'd get a feel for the type of appropriate touch that goes along with babies. We'd hold a pillow like we were holding one of the boys, and we'd lightly pet it like we were petting a miniature dog and say, "See Avery? Gennnntle ... Gennnntle. Now you try." We'd put the pillow in her lap, and she'd mimic us perfectly (again, she's strategic like this). Then—because she begged and begged and begged, "I want to hold him!"—we'd delicately place one of the boys in her lap, and in the blink of an eye, she'd do Jiu-Jitsu on his face (or, the Secret Art of the White Tiger). Honestly, it was amazing. I'm quite confident that due to her premium intelligence, she knows there are only a handful of years available, a small window of time, before they will have the upper hand and overpower her (again, it's the strategy).

So after saying "GENTLE" for the four hundreth time, we finally took a different approach—at least for a period of time. No longer could Avery hold one of the boys. No longer could we as parents EVER allow Avery to be alone in a room with the boys. NEVER can she be allowed to feed the boys ANYTHING ... One particular day when the boys were almost one, I walked out of the living room and into the bathroom for maybe sixty seconds. When I walked back into the living room, Jude was gag reflexing repeatedly, trying desperately to get whatever was lodged in his throat out. His face was a vibrant mixed shade of red and purple hews. Immediately, I did what I've had to do several times and what I hate doing! I stuck my finger down his throat to dislodge what had to be forty-eight Cheerios.

And right then and there, a new rule had to be created. So I stooped down and pulled Avery up next to me and said, "Avery, let's ONLY allow Mommy and Daddy to feed the boys, okay?" And although this seems like the obvious conversation, truthfully, this was a difficult thing to say. For a two-year-old *to share* in our house would be nothing short of a miracle. It would be akin to the parting of the Red Sea or Lazarus being raised from the dead. And that's exactly what she thought she was doing—sharing. On top of that, she loves playing "a motherly role" with her little brothers, which makes me think the twins won't be raised by two parents, but three.

All that to say, at the age of two, Avery didn't have the mental equipment to understand why she shouldn't feed the boys. She didn't have the mental capacity to understand the potentially tragic effects it could have if she were to feed the twins something unbeknownst to us, her parents. So at a young age, there are and have been several situations that called for Avery to simply obey her parents. *Simple, straight-forward obedience* was the best mode of relationship between her and us, and that's been a healthy thing. In fact, I'd say the majority of Avery's life as a two-year-old was learned by way of simple, straight-forward obedience. That is, we never allowed input from her as to what she should wear in a given day or what she should eat for breakfast, lunch, or dinner. Otherwise, she'd run around naked at all times and eat fruit roll-ups and cheese sticks three times a day. So when she was two, her input would probably not have provided the wisest alternatives. That's why these decisions were provided for her. And believe me, that is the BEST mode of operation when dealing with a two-year-old.

However, imagine this: Someday Avery will no longer be a toddler as she is now. Someday she will be sixteen, seventeen, and eighteen. And let's just say, hypothetically speaking, that two days ago, I drew up a concise little contract four pages in length that states she cannot date until she is twenty-five. Hypothetically speaking, of course. And let's just say that she scribbled on the dotted line what appears to be her name in purple crayon. It looks more like the state of Delaware, but my attorney friends tell me it will hold up in court. So all is good.

And somehow, someway, we arrive at the age of twenty, and she is begging to go out on her first date. Okay, okay. Perhaps that is unrealistic. How about, we arrive at the age of eighteen and she is begging to go out on her first date? No? Okay, she's sixteen, and that's as low as I'm gonna go. I whip out the contract that's been filed away for just such an occasion and dismissively tell her, "There's no conversation to be had, and the next time we'll revisit this conversation is when you're twenty-five." The conversation lasts all of four seconds. Right.

Now that should go over swimmingly. And the reason that's a laughable scenario is because I've just treated my sixteen-year-old like a two-year-old. Come to think of it, there was actually more conversation created between her and me over not feeding the boys when she was two than going out on a date fourteen years later. Not only that, but can you imagine the crippling effects this would have on her emotional, mental, and social well-being if I were to try to stick to this erroneous contract? In other words, my mode of parenting as a father will evolve as she grows older.

At the age of two, there were times when simple, straight-forward obedience without conversation was called for, because she had neither the mental equipment nor the maturity to understand the full ramifications of her actions. But I'm taking a shot in the dark by guessing that she will require more conversation and more argument at the age of sixteen. Simple, dismissive obedience won't do. And it shouldn't. Parents of teenagers may disagree, but the maturity of a sixteen-year-old is not at the same level as a two-year-old.

I recall leadership class readings in college that suggested something of the same thing—that the lowest levels of management (or leadership) found in unhealthy organizations frequently played the "obedience card," while healthier organizations bred greater levels of *conversation* between the management and its employees. And it makes sense, doesn't it? If the management of a company only demands obedience out of its employees and never allows opportunity for an employee's personality and creative freedom to be accessed, the employees are simply reduced to robots. Never will the employees mature and develop professionally, and the company will suffer.

Likewise, there will be a day when my daughter is allowed to date. And in all probability, I'll not play the obedience card and demand she not date until she's twenty-five. But we *will have* numerous conversations about the types of guys worth dating and the types of guys not worth dating. And let's be clear on this—somewhere down the road, she will be the one who chooses whom to date, although that doesn't mean she will make perfect choices, either.

If she's like most humans, she will make some poor choices on more than one occasion. She will most likely experience heartbreak and could even experience betrayal. I mean, what if some idiot fifteen-year-old male who's just hit puberty in stride has decided he'd rather take some other girl to the dance twenty-four hours beforehand? Or, what if some drunk hormonal imbecile tries to take advantage of her? To even imagine some jerk down the road mistreating my little girl can send me into a nice little rage-filled wonderland. Momentarily, I've trailed off into an anger fantasy that has me playing Jet Li with some teenage boy's face, and all of a sudden, this has become a little more difficult to type.

This is stupid! Just as my fingertips are hitting the keypad, I've ignorantly let myself wander off into a world of pain that hasn't even taken place! And still, do you know what would be *worse*? What would be worse would be for *me* to choose who she dates. What would be worse would be for *me* to dictate to her which friends to have and which not to have. What would be worse would be for *me* to dictate which career she pursues. Because then, she would forever remain a two-year-old, and I would be her codependent father.

In truth, there *will* be days ahead when I'll experience a depth of pain I've never before experienced. Her life will be rocked by a relationship abruptly cut off. Her world will come unraveled after experiencing failure for the very first time. She'll not find her way into some organization or another of which she really wanted to be a part, and her entire sense of self will come undone. And because she is mine, her pain will awaken parts of me I never knew existed.

And do you know where I'll want to be? *There.* With her. Fully present. Nowhere else.

Nothing will occupy my mind and soul more than those moments. And if allowed the chance to be there with her, no other moment will be more sacred than that. In fact, that's all I can promise her. As a father, I can't promise her a life without pain, and I can't promise her 100 percent success. But I can promise her my presence. And even though I offer my presence, that doesn't necessarily mean the offer will be taken up.

1. *The American Heritage Dictionary of the English Language*, 4th Ed., (Houghton Mifflin Company: 2000).

2. J.B. Phillips, *Your God Is Too Small* (Touchstone Books, New York, NY: 1997) p. 21.

PART 4

ALTERNATIVE 3:

KINGDOM

"Even in your hobbies, has there not always been ... something, not to be identified with, but always on the verge of breaking through, the smell of cut wood in the workshop or the clap-clap of water against the boat's side? Are not all lifelong friendships born at the moment when at last you meet another human being who has some inkling (but faint and uncertain even in the best) of that something which you were born desiring, and which, beneath the flux of other desires and in all the momentary silences between the louder passions, night and day, year by year, from childhood to old age, you are looking for, watching for, listening for?"

—C.S. Lewis

11

CHAPTER

THE PRIMARY MESSAGE
OF JESUS

So far, the metaphors of *discipleship* and *fatherhood* have retooled
our overall approach to decision-making, not just the actual
process of choosing a career or potential date or new church,
but also our expectations and end-goals. We've left behind
formulas, recipes, treasure maps, and blueprints in lieu of other
metaphors like *discipleship, fatherhood,* and now *kingdom.* "God's
will as a formula to be deciphered" smacks of an intricate
configuration of variables that's practically *intended* to confuse.
No doubt, many people today feel as though their lives are lived
inside a maze, and God is the one who's placed them there.
Since they've experienced so much confusion in life, they have
naturally envisioned God to be the one who authors all the
confusion when, in fact, the opposite image of God is portrayed
in the Scriptures!

The sort of God depicted in the Scriptures is one of availability
rather than confusion and secrecy. "Look at Me. I stand at the

door. I knock. If you hear me call and open the door, I'll come right in and sit down to supper with you" (Revelations 3:20 The Message). In fact, John 1 conveys a Jesus who is present in our world in a most profound way:

> The Life-Light was the real thing:
> Every person entering Life
> he brings into Light.
> *He was in the world,*
> *the world was there through him,*
> *and yet the world didn't even notice.*
> He came to his own people,
> but they didn't want him.
> But whoever did want him,
> who believed he was who he claimed
> and would do what he said,
> He made to be their true selves,
> their child-of-God selves.
> These are the God-begotten,
> not blood-begotten,
> not flesh-begotten,
> not sex-begotten.
> *The Word became flesh and blood,*
> *and moved into the neighborhood.*
> We saw the glory with our own eyes,
> the one-of-a-kind glory,
> like Father, like Son,
> Generous inside and out,
> true from start to finish.
> (John 1:1-14 The Message, emphasis mine)

Never does it seem as though God has intently set out to confuse those whom He's created, and yet the idea of formulas, treasure maps, and blueprints has damaged so many individuals who truly desire to make God-centered decisions. Instead, they've become completely disoriented due to the stress and ambiguity formulas create.

I've certainly been in that place of confusion in the past, where I've actually become *more confused* by trying to sincerely ask myself, "Am I operating on my desires or God's desires? Is my direction lining up with His?" Years ago, I found myself bogged down with a particular decision when a friend sent this prayer to me by Thomas Merton, a twentieth-century monk and poet. Since that time, I've come back to this prayer several times over, because no matter what stage of decision-making I've found myself in, I've connected with it on one level or another.

> My Lord God,
> I have no idea where I am going.
>
> I do not see the road ahead of me
> Nor do I really know myself,
> And the fact that I think I am following your will
> Does not mean that I am actually doing so.
> But I believe that the desire to please you
> Does in fact please you.
>
> And I hope that I will never do anything apart from that desire.
> And I know that if I do this,
> You will lead me by the right road
> Though I may know nothing about it.
>
> Therefore will I trust you always,
> Though I may seem to be lost and in the shadow of death.
> I will not fear, for you are ever with me,
> And you will never leave me to face my struggles alone.
> Thomas Merton, 1915–1968

Maybe it's echoed my sentiments because I feel a sense of root-ed-ness in honestly admitting the fact that I usually can't "see the road ahead of me," and in that admission, a greater level of trust is birthed. Or maybe it's echoed my sentiments because his prayer has brought me back to question my assumptions, moti-vations, and possible illusions—"And the fact that I think I am following your will does not mean that I am actually doing so." Or maybe his prayer has become mine so often because there's been a sense of reassurance felt when stating, "But I believe that the desire to please you does in fact please you." Or maybe it's all of the above.

As we move into our final section, the metaphor of *kingdom* is perhaps one more indication that it has never been God's desire to create complications around the subject matter of God's will. Again, God is a God of availability, not confusion and secrecy. Just as *fatherhood* empowers us to take responsibility for our lives and make decisions for ourselves, *kingdom* follows through by giving us further direction in the actual process of decision-making ... in other words, how to actually choose one path over another with the confidence of God's support.

A POLL

If you polled ten different individuals and asked them, "Where should the local Church in America concentrate its efforts in the coming years?" Depending on each individual's personality, convictions, history, readings, and experiences, you could very well receive ten different responses. Some could be:

- The Church must move beyond maintaining numbers and address future generations, or it will become extinct in fifty years;

- The Church must address the AIDS epidemic in Africa

that's well on its way to surpassing the devastating effects of the bubonic plague of the Middle Ages;

- The Church should address the deteriorated inner cities and needs of the impoverished and marginalized;

- The Church should concentrate its efforts in sending local representatives globally to further its mission;

- The Church has to be a refuge for families and married couples, because, certainly, today's culture has been hard-wired for attacking the sanctity of the home;

- The Church must be sensitive to and care for the elderly, for they're the ones who've paved the road we're walking on;

- The Church should spend its time creating a wide variety of artistic platforms in order to connect with a wide variety of people in today's culture; and more ...

After hearing each response, could anyone actually say, "No! That's ridiculous! What a waste of time to invest in future generations ... or sub-Saharan Africa ... or caring for the elderly ... or preserving marriages and families ... or reaching out to the impoverished and marginalized!" Hopefully, you wouldn't hear such a rejection of these various missions, because the necessity of each is obvious.

In the same way, if you polled ten different individuals and asked them, "What is the message of Jesus Christ?" depending on each individual's personality, convictions, history, readings, and experiences, you could very well receive ten different responses. Some could be:

- The message of Jesus Christ is grace—short and simple—grace;

- The message of Jesus is that He enables us to live life after death;

- The message of Jesus is liberation in that He liberates the oppressed;

- The message of Jesus is holiness in that He instills and enables us to live lives of holiness;

- The message of Jesus is found in giving distinction and glory to God;

- The message of Jesus is that He heals the scarred and broken;

- The message of Jesus is atonement in that Jesus has repaired the way for humans to have relationship with God; and more ...

Again, after hearing each response, could anyone actually say, "No! That's ridiculous! Jesus' message had nothing to do with grace, but liberation." Or, "Jesus' message had nothing to do with healing, but God's glory!" Hopefully, we would be able to hear each of these descriptions and immediately see the necessity of each one in trying to describe all that Jesus embodied. Typically, our problems in describing Jesus come when we try to paint Jesus with just one brush in just one color. In truth, Jesus is and has always been gracious, holy, atoning, eternal, liberating, healing, forgiving, and much more. In fact, the older I've become, the more I've realized how constricting I've been in trying to confine God with my one-sided, one-dimensional perspective.

But test-drive this: Could every facet of Jesus' message be found in this simple, almost mysterious phrase, "*the kingdom of God*"? Whether it be grace, God's glory, healing, forgiveness, liberation, eternity, or atonement, could *all of it* be consumed in the simple statement found time and time again on the lips of Jesus in the first century, "The kingdom of God is at hand" (Mark 1:15 NASB)? In fact, it's interesting that the Gospel of Mark cuts to the chase in the very first chapter and immediately explains just what Jesus had come to do. "Now after John had been taken into custody, Jesus came into Galilee, preaching the gospel of God, and saying, 'The time is fulfilled, and the kingdom of God is at hand; repent and believe in the gospel'" (Mark 1:14-15 NASB).

The kingdom of God. What in the world is that? Well, in the spirit of Dallas Willard, it's simply the ruling and reigning of God—the place where what God wants to see happen in lives, relationships, societies, or situations actually happens. The reason this phrase initially sounds so ambiguous is because "kingdom" had all sorts of mileage two thousand years ago that it doesn't today. Two thousand years ago, the word "kingdom" was a commonplace expression describing the reign of Julius Caesar in Rome. Today, though, is a different story. "Kingdom" isn't the word we citizens use when referring to states or countries and is rarely heard in everyday conversation. Nevertheless, the message and reality of what Jesus was trying to communicate is the same whether you're talking about 14 A.D. or 2014 A.D. "The kingdom of God" is simply the place where God's desires become tangible.

The kingdom of God happens when medical supplies find their way into the hands of a grandfather who's doctoring his AIDS-infected son in Zambia. The kingdom of God happens when an elderly widow's house in the inner city is renovated without a cent of her own money. It happens when a thirty-six-year-old married man is greeted with the opportunity of infidelity but chooses against the advice of his impulses. It happens when a forty-eight-year-old man searching for recognition and achievement discovers grace for the very first time. And it happens when an eight-year-old Russian orphan experiences value and worth for the very first time.

The kingdom of God happens today when a teenage girl takes ownership over her life and pulls herself out of an abusive relationship. The kingdom of God happens when a family blindsided by tragedy is overwhelmed by the support and empathy of their friends. The kingdom of God happens when a person who's been wronged chooses forgiveness rather than vengeance. It happens when porn addicts take steps toward releasing their addiction. And it happens when a husband and wife take steps toward ending years of damaging conversation that's become their marriage norm.

The kingdom of God is taking place all around us at this very second, and obviously, there is a sense in which the kingdom of God doesn't just happen on its own accord. It doesn't just *appear*, like "Voila!" No, it is actually quite real and takes place because people have taken it upon themselves to bring about change, either in their own lives or in their surroundings.

KINGDOM: TWO ASPECTS TO GOD'S WILL

Now I hate to resort to foolish banter (or continue along the path of foolish banter, depending on your take), but there's a fair chance the kingdom of God has an actual king. This king could be the one identified by the prepositional phrase "*of God.*" So let's imagine this king for a few moments: Does this king have a will for his citizens? You bet he does. Brian McLaren, in his article "Across the Great Decide," says, "He doesn't want them killing each other, stealing one another's cattle, building faulty bridges or buildings, or cooperating with the enemies of the kingdom." In other words, in striving to understand God's will, there is a sense in which the metaphor of kingdom applies to all of us equally, because we're all striving to be citizens of the kingdom. But the will of the king doesn't end there. McLaren goes on to describe other ways a king's will applies to his subjects:

> Ok, you say, but these areas apply to everyone equally. Are there any ways that a king has a will for an individual? Of course. If you are the best lute player in the land, and the king has a special feast coming up, I'm sure it's his will for you to come and play the lute. And if you're the best boat-builder in the land, he'd like you to build some great boats for the kingdom. He'd rather the lute-player not build boats, and vice versa.[1]

So the metaphor of kingdom exemplifies two aspects of God's will: a *general will* that applies to everyone equally, and a *specific will* that applies to everyone individually. Certainly, the king knows that His citizens are most fulfilled when utilizing their abilities. That's why the king has a specific will for each individual that ensures his abilities are accessed. The question to consider, then, is, "How far does the king's specific will extend?" When discussing the king's specific will, we must realize that *it is at this very place* that treasure maps, recipes, and blueprints are birthed. Are we saying that the king holds a detailed blueprint that delineates "to the 'T'" how each citizen should spend every second of every day? "Today, I'd first like you to go to the grocery store. Then to the coffeehouse. Then work. Then the gym—and not the gym *before* work, but *after* work." Of course not. As McLaren says, "He is a king, not a puppet-master." But keep in mind, whether we're talking about the king's general will or specific will, his ultimate aim is the good of the kingdom! And no matter how each of us employs the king's specific will for our lives, if we can't connect it with the good of the kingdom, then we'll most likely not experience the full meaning for which our lives were intended.

If we employ our abilities as accountants, then we ought to do all we can to be the best, most honorable accountants we could possibly be—and to connect the very act of accounting with the kingdom itself! And if we employ our abilities as actors, then we ought to do all we can to be the best, most honorable actors we could possibly be—and to connect the very act of acting with the kingdom itself! And if we employ our abilities as doctors, then we ought to do all we can to be the best, most honorable doctors we could possibly be—and to connect the very practice of medicine to the kingdom itself. In fact, because we believe that God is the one who gave us these abilities in the first place and is the ultimate creator of these arts, then we ought to hold our jobs with a sense of sacredness and distinction. We should treat others with a sense of dignity and respect, while also maintaining an acute sense of discernment about our mission. In essence, we should never forget that the will of the king for every life exists for the good of the kingdom.

'THE THING I WAS MADE FOR'

In today's day and age, I wish the question of what you should do with your life was as easy as choosing among four options. As our world and technology have developed through the years, so have the multitude of career options. In *The Problem of Pain*, C.S. Lewis says:

> All the things that have ever deeply possessed your soul have been but hints of it, tantalizing glimpses, promises never quite fulfilled, echoes that died away just as they caught your ear. But if it should really become manifest—if there ever came an echo that did not die away but swelled

into the sound itself—you would know it. Beyond all possibility of doubt you would say "Here at last is the thing I was made for."[2]

Yes! I know exactly what Lewis speaks of! I have had and still have this life-giving thing that communicates with my soul. It happens when I've caught a seventy-four-degree cloudless day, and I'm standing with a pair of Nike Tiempo Premiers on my feet, beneath which is a lush, green Bermuda tiff pitch. The height of this grass is no more than four inches, and a great group of guys have assembled to play soccer. And there—*right there*—in the middle of strategy, sweat, and the rhythm of the game, I am caught up into another world. *"Here at last is the thing I was made for."*

So why am I not playing for Real Madrid? I'll tell you why. Because I'm not that good. I mean, don't get me wrong, I'm incredible—about as incredible as someone who could play in a local recreational city league.

And I'm probably not alone in my experience. I mean, the majority of us are people who have a diversity of interests. Therefore, if asked the question—"what is the thing you were made for?"—our lives might begin to look a bit blurry. We have several desires and many interests; sometimes, we're just not entirely sure which one should provide our salary. Or which interest holds enough weight to devote thousands and thousands of dollars in schooling and living expenses?

At this level, I think it is here that our friends should earn their keep.

"Jason, you know how much I love music. I am thinking of taking my show on the road, moving to Seattle, finding an apartment, and trying 'to make it.' I need you to be honest with me. You've heard my stuff. Do you think this would be a wise decision?"

"Honestly?"
"Yes, honestly."
"What do you mean by 'honestly'?"
"You know, 'honestly'!"

"When you say, 'honestly,' do you mean 'honestly' as it's described in Webster's Revised Unabridged Dictionary?"

"Probably ... well, I don't know. Just tell me exactly what is in your head at this very second and tell it as though thousands and thousands of dollars depend on it. Because it does."

"Okay, I will tell you, but first let me ask you a preliminary question that will dictate my response ... will we still be friends after I say exactly what is in my head?"

"Umm. Nevermind. I think I'm hearing what you're saying."
"Really? Has it taken you this long?"

Truly, our friends could and should play a significant role here. And still, just because we pursue one career vocationally, does that mean our other interests can't be accessed in our off-time or play a role in our lives' fulfillment? For some, it might be fairly liberating to shed the expectation that *one* particular career will completely satisfy every longing, dream, or ability that we've ever possessed. Certainly, Western culture has typically rotated around vocation, but our lives are far too sacred to be defined so narrowly.

Today, the two dominant questions from which we derive a sense of identity are: "What is your name?" and "What do you do?" How, then, would I respond? Well, my name is Kyle, and what do I do? I am a husband. And I am a father. I also pastor a church that goes by the name, UBC, but it's really just a humorous bunch of people who are trying to understand and experience God in genuine ways. Somehow in the midst of pastoring, these people probably provide a greater sense of identity for me than my actual title does. I also enjoy playing very sub-par soccer in a very sub-par league on very sub-par fields that I wish would be renovated. It seems the outdoors is as much a part of who I am as almost anything.

In other words, there's quite a bit that goes into understanding who you are. And, an important part of the journey toward understanding who you are lies in identifying the vast number of different components at play there. Though my annual salary comes from my occupation as a pastor, pastoring doesn't hold the monopoly on my identity as a person. It's what I do, but my life couldn't possibly be summarized by the word, "pastor." This is an important distinction to be made in embracing the sense of sacredness our lives hold, and it's an important distinction to be made when identifying potential career possibilities. *Your identity extends beyond vocation.*

Several factors are involved in identifying potential locations in the workforce. Who you are amounts to much more than just particular talents and abilities. Your past experiences certainly play a significant role in shaping your identity. As well, there could be a particular demographic of people with whom you enjoy connecting, whether it be eighty-four-year-old stroke patients or eight-year-old inner city kids. Or, maybe who you are doesn't have as much to do with demographics as it does a particular product—like building homes or repairing cars. Or, maybe who you are has its ties to the family business. There could be a great sense of tradition involved in holding a particular job in which a significant amount of meaning is found in decades of history in a particular service.

No doubt, a vast number of things play a part in defining your particular uniqueness. And the fact that right now, I'm trying to figure out a simple recipe to summarize your existence echoes the very heart of this book—it can't and never will be neatly bow-tied. "Just take two parts past experience mixed with four parts talent and six parts classroom teaching and there we are ... a fulfilling, meaningful life! Rather, a single human life—mind, body, spirit, and soul—is too intricate and wonderfully fashioned to be reduced to a recipe for meaning. And still, assessments aimed at discovering your abilities, giftedness, and mode of being are very helpful! Many of these assessments can be found online and could play a key role in helping you understand some of who you are and how you operate. For example, the Meyers-Briggs personality assessment is one that I'd recommend to anyone. Along these lines, several worthwhile questions to consider are:

- What past experiences have significantly shaped your life perspectives and future desires? These experiences could be circumstances, a job or internship, a key individual met along the way, or even tragedy.

- How does your mind operate? Do you flourish in contexts where you're given clearly defined to-do's on a weekly or monthly basis, or where you're given plenty of space to create (or somewhere in between)? A great deal of fulfillment or frustration can be found in this single area alone.

- Do particular demographics of people play a major role in your sense of direction? These could include teen moms, orphaned kids, the elderly, college students, the impoverished, middle-aged businessmen and women, high school students, young married couples, etc.

Again, you could have several simultaneous interests.

- In what abilities have you shown competence and potential? A few broad examples that apply to a wealth of opportunities include teaching, leading, designing, creating, repairing, calculating, communicating, administrating, performing ... Certainly, you can be particularly detailed in the area of abilities, but these listed here seem to provide the launching pad from which most abilities spring.

1. Brian McLaren, "Across the Great Decide," *Christian Single* magazine, *www. christiansingle.com*, accessed June 12, 2002.

2. C.S. Lewis, *The Problem of Pain* (Harper Collins, New York, NY: 1940) p. 60.

12
CHAPTER

A YEAR AND A HALF?

We've already explored some ways "the general will" applies to each of us, namely that God desires us to be gracious, forgiving, discerning, self-controlled, compassionate people rather than angry, embittered, jealous, hateful people. And why? Because God's desire is that we all experience the very best kind of life there is to live. And I know from experience that it's so much more freeing to forgive someone for a wrong done to me than to allow that wrongdoing to fester and bleed bitterness throughout my entire self. Bitterness *is not* the way to live. I also know from experience that a life rooted in God's grace and unconditional love entails a lot less stress, anxiety, and constant people-pleasing than a life hinged on its own performance and achievements.

So it's evident that the King has a general will that applies to all of His citizens equally—a desire for the citizens of the kingdom to experience the fullest life there is to live. But let's now turn our attention to exploring the King's *specific will* in greater depth.

Most of us in life aren't born with the knowledge that we are lute players or boat builders. Okay, yes, I've heard of some very successful people who seemed to know they wanted to be a dentist or home builder or hotel manager or doctor or pharmacist or veterinarian ever since they were two. "Oh yes," they say. "I remember discovering *exactly* what I wanted to do with my life after rounding the bases in a game of kickball at recess in Mrs. Thompson's first-grade class!" And frankly, these people need to be kicked very hard in a most un-Christian-like manner.

The vast majority of us were not born with the knowledge that we are lute players or boat builders. We weren't born with the knowledge of what we wanted to be, or who we wanted to marry, or where we wanted to live—although I wish we were. If it were up to me, I'd rather roll out of bed one day with the knowledge and expertise in either: a) lute playing or b) boat building. I'd rather not try my hand at the lute, screw up, and look like the idiot just to eliminate lute playing from the endless list of possibilities.

In my second year of college, I dated a particular girl who lived about ten minutes from campus. One particular Spring evening, I had left my place and was driving over to hers for a date. I recall this particular drive vividly because it was in the span of those ten minutes that the first light bulb came on. I can even tell you what I was listening to in the car—"Patience" off the Guns N' Roses album *Lies*. I was whistling and brainstorming at the same time because I am a multi-tasker. Actually, that's about as much as I can do simultaneously, so I guess that doesn't make me a multi-tasker, but a dual-tasker.

The entire drive over, I was brainstorming conversation topics that could possibly take us through the entire date from beginning to end. "Alright, as soon as we finish talking about this, then we can talk about *this*, then *this*, and *this* ..." Something tells me this isn't quite normal. Perhaps it could be if this is a first date and you've got a lot of anxiety, but this was not our first date. We had been going out *a year and a half.*

Okay, so I'm a little slow. Or a lot slow. There is, in fact, a formulaic equation for just such a scenario. I don't know if this equation has been researched or well-documented, but if not, let this be the first. I'm fairly confident a high percentage of both males and females will agree. First, consider what's involved here:

Fact #1—Males are stereotypically visual beings.

Fact #2—The level of an individual male's depth is directly proportional to the amount of use he has over his thought processes in the presence of a pleasant-looking female.

Fact #3—All other variables aside, looks alone can sustain a male's participation in a relationship anywhere from two weeks to four months.

So after applying the facts of my scenario to the equation, the equation is as follows:

$$\begin{array}{c} \textbf{Good-looking female} \\ + \\ \textbf{Visually-stimulated male} \\ - \\ \textbf{Male's thought processes} \\ = \\ \textbf{Length of dating relationship (if described in increments} \\ \textbf{of time—seventeen months in my case)} \end{array}$$

The beauty of this equation is found in its flexibility ... if you transferred the increments from time to feet, you could also find out the actual intellectual and emotional depth of the male under examination:

Good-looking female

+

Visually-stimulated male

-

Male's thought processes

=

Actual intellectual & emotional depth of male (if described in increments of feet—0.2 feet in my case)

So let's consider the fact that looks alone can sustain the guy's participation in the relationship anywhere from two weeks to four months—*and*—the fact that my relationship with this particular girl lasted a year and a half. Evidently, then, my intellectual and emotional depth measured somewhere in the vicinity of a kiddy pool. The dimly lit bulb in my head made me think, "This is weird. We've been dating for over a year now. Should I be pulling teeth just to hold conversation with my girlfriend of over a year?" The fact that this thought came at month seventeen and not month one is telling. Sure, maybe it's not uncommon to have conversation hurdles with an individual in the first five days of dating, but not the 450th.

You know the cliché regarding "true love"?—That couples in love can sit in silence together and not feel pressured to fill the space with words? I think that legendary saying assumes that at one time, some significant conversation existed in the first place!

A couple of weeks later, I was around my family when the dimly lit bulb grew even brighter. I found myself showcasing my girlfriend to my family as if I worked at a used car lot. "You'll want to notice her eyes of pearl ... Don't you think she is quite the looker? And did I mention her premium intelligence?" Somewhere in the middle of my salesmanship, these thoughts drifted into my head, "Why am I having to sell my girlfriend to my family? My family is made up of really good people. It's not like they're in the mafia. So, shouldn't her identity speak for itself? And shouldn't our compatibility speak for itself? Hmmm ... this is weird."

Slowly but surely, the bulb was finally pulled to its brightest and within the next month, we broke up. After *a year and a half* of dating, we finally broke up. Wow. And the number one thing I repeatedly said to myself after the breakup was, "What a waste of time! What a mistake! I spent a year and a half of my life just to eliminate one more girl from the sea of marriage possibilities. What a waste of time. What a mistake."

According to my formulaic, blueprint depiction of God's will, I didn't end that relationship feeling entirely relieved, I ended that relationship feeling *more* anxiety and more stress about my future. One of the things a couple of different people said after our breakup was, "Don't worry, Kyle. There are a lot more fish in the sea than her." Obviously, this statement was meant to comfort, and it did at some level. When coming off a breakup, it's nice to be reminded of the fact that there are tons of other possibilities out there than this single person you just dated. But when you're carrying around an image in your head of God's will as a treasure map, "a lot more fish in the sea" can create a lot more stress, anxiety, and uncertainty about your future. According to the treasure map, "a lot more fish in the sea" can be a reminder that among the billions of fish out there, you haven't found *the right one*! And that's exactly the way I felt.

TRADING CLICHÉ FOR MEANING

Naturally, when overcome by the anxiety of failure and disap-pointment, our next step is to project our anxieties and frustration on God and question, "God, what are YOU doing with my life? Why are You doing this to me? Don't You care about my future and my desires for (insert your dilemma here)?" You certainly hear these kinds of prayers offered throughout the Psalms, and there's something healthy about communicating our innermost thoughts and feelings—creating total openness with God. But keep in mind, understanding God's will through the metaphor of *fatherhood* has helped us take responsibility for the people we date—and not just the people we date, but the jobs, colleges, churches, friends, and locations we choose in life. Also, understanding God's will through the metaphor of *discipleship* has helped remind us that God has never promised an easy life free of disappointment and pain.

In fact, I wonder if this is the actual sentiment behind the oft repeated prayer, "God, I place this situation in Your hands ..." When we hear or say those words, what is actually being communicated there? What are we intending to say? Recently, I was driving to an important meeting and voiced these very words in the car. I had been feeling apprehensive about this particular meeting for several days. So on the drive over, I began talking to God about it, and almost without thought, I voiced, "God, I place this meeting in Your hands." Almost simultaneously, in the midst of realizing the clichéd vibe of my conversation with God, I immediately questioned, "Wait, what do I mean by that?" I've prayed those very words for years and years, but I think my feelings about that phrase have changed over time—from what I meant by that phrase five years ago to what I mean by that phrase now.

I'm quite certain this questioning threw God for a loop. He must have thrown His hands in the air in complete disbelief and confusion saying, "Alright, Lake, when you get your thoughts together, call Me; but until then, I don't want to hear a word."

Rather than allowing myself to continue on the path of usual conversation with God, I stopped to process my words and motives to God aloud:

> God, when I say, "I place this meeting in Your hands," You know that I don't expect this meeting to come off without a hitch just because I've "given it to You." I know that Your involvement in my life doesn't guarantee unwavering success, and it certainly doesn't guarantee that things will turn out just as I want them to. There are other people involved here who may have entirely different views and hopes than me.

> God, Your thoughts and Your ways are far beyond mine.

> You are probably aware of what I want to see happen here. I really hope we'll get on the other side of this meeting, and everyone will be on the same page. And if there are disagreements, I hope they'll be worked out smoothly. But God, I know that's not always the way things turn out. Help me do my part in creating a constructive environment and to communicate clearly, respectfully, and with definite boundaries.

> I guess, in the end, what I'm saying is that I'm not placing this meeting in Your hands just so I don't have to take responsibility for how it turns out. And I'm also not placing this meeting in Your hands just to finagle the outcome I want.

But I do know You have my best interests in mind, and that You're not working against me, but for me. So help me keep trusting You and Your desires for my life.

An important rite of passage for any follower of Christ takes place when we force our words to have meaning—even if meaningful conversation with God consists of ten words. Certainly, in conversation with God, it's important we know the meaning of our words. And wow, doesn't that sound like rocket science. I've always had a knack for stating the obvious, and there I go again ... In conversation with God, it's important we know the meaning of our words. This applies when praying through a particular decision or opportunity, but truthfully, this applies when praying through anything.

Jesus says something of the sort when communicating His legendary "Sermon on the Mount," the single greatest sermon that turned first-century views of religion on their head. In Matthew 6, Jesus says:

> And when you come before God, don't turn that into a theatrical production either. All these people making a regular show out of their prayers, hoping for stardom! Do you think God sits in a box seat?

> Here's what I want you to do: Find a quiet, secluded place so you won't be tempted to role-play before God. Just be there as simply and honestly as you can manage. The focus will shift from you to God, and you will begin to sense his grace.

> The world is full of so-called prayer warriors who are prayer-ignorant. *They're full of formulas and programs and advice, peddling techniques for getting what you want from God.* Don't fall for that nonsense. This is your Father

you are dealing with, and he knows better than you what you need." (Matthew 6:5-12 The Message, emphasis mine)

As we move away from a formulaic understanding of God's will, it's imperative we take a second look at the way we approach God in prayer. Prayer is one of the vehicles through which we understand God and God's direction for our lives, so we must beware that prayer itself could be used as a short-cut to get what we want from God.

Through the years, I've actually seen a few different aspects of the Christian life uprooted and rewritten to get what we want from God. Prayer is not the only one. Even in the Christian life, there are other spiritual disciplines that have been rewritten to insure a particular desired outcome. Tithing is one of them.

Tithing is another integral aspect of the Christian life that can be reframed in formulaic ways. For instance, I recently heard it suggested that if you faithfully tithe to God, *God will give back to you tenfold*. And God's "giving back" was definitely described in lucrative terms. Anyone, then, could naturally hear this sermon and respond, "Okay! I'll tithe!" I mean, who ever got to a place in life where they said, "You know, I sure have gotten tired of having so much money!" No. Naturally, anyone could hear this sermon and immediately tithe, but, in the process, entirely miss the point of tithing.

The point of tithing is that it's a tangible way of naming the ultimate owner of all things. I recognize that God is the one who gave me the breath, ability, brain, and creativity to own my job in the first place. So I strive to approach my job and money with a sense of sacredness, understanding God to be the ultimate source of my ability to earn money. With that in mind, doesn't it sound as though our approach to tithing becomes perverted once we say, "If you faithfully tithe to God, He will give back to you tenfold"?

Now, what in the world does this have to do with God's will? Well, is the point of tithing—or— the point of prayer—or—the point of deciphering God's will—or—the point of following Christ, so that we get something in return? More money. Less chaos. A smoother life. Less resistance. More future certainty. Less future risk. More health. Less illness.

Maybe a question "God's will" keeps placing before us is, "What do we expect from God?" Because if we expect God to rescue us from a life of risk, disappointment, and failure, then maybe that's an indication that we're not taking seriously enough our process of discipleship. Or, if we expect God to take responsibility for the decisions *we* make, then maybe that's an indication that we want God to be much more than a Father—also a dictator or tyrant.

POOR CHOICES, WISE CHOICES, AND ROAD RAGE

Now, in light of my overdue breakup, let's turn our attention toward answering this question, "What distinguishes a wise decision from a poor one?" Even though the decision to date that particular girl ended in disappointment, was dating her a bad decision? Keep in mind that I'm not asking, "Was dating her *seventeen months* a good decision?!" That's another story that I don't care to get into again. So how can we differentiate poor choices from wise ones?

In his foreword to an insightful book written years ago, Haddon Robinson said:

> When we ask, "How can I know the will of God?" we may be raising a pagan question. In the ancient world

kings and generals consulted the oracles to gain guidance from the gods for their plans. The oracles provided such direction by vague and illusive counsel and worshipers could read into the enigmatic responses what their hunches told them to do. Convinced that their plans had the stamp of the gods, generals could lead their troops into battle with unfounded courage. By 300 B.C., however, the oracles had gone out of business. Too often they had led their devotees to staggering defeat.

> If we ask, "How can I know the will of God?" we may be asking the wrong question. The Scriptures do not command us to find God's will for most of life's choices nor do we have any passage instructing us on how it can be determined. Equally significant, the Christian community has never agreed on how God provides us with such special revelation. Yet we persist in searching for God's will because decisions require thought and sap energy ... Instead of wondering, "How do I find the will of God?" a better question to pursue is, "How do I make good decisions?"[1]

That is the question, then, that I want to address—the difference between a good decision and a bad one. In light of our discussion thus far, if we evaluate our decisions based on their outcomes, who could decipher which decisions were wise and which were poor? Some very good decisions in life end in disappointment, and oddly enough, some of the worst decisions made in life turn out beautifully. Therefore, it becomes even more imperative that we project our decisions against the backdrop of *discipleship, fatherhood,* and *kingdom.*

I'll answer this question, then, like this: One Tuesday morning months ago, three friends and I were scheduled to travel to Austin to catch a flight to San Diego. Oddly enough, we woke up that morning to an iced-over Central Texas, something that doesn't happen too often. Before leaving the house that morning, this was the decision we had to make:

Option A: Drive from Waco to try to make our Austin flight. At the time we called, the flights out of Austin were on-schedule, but we were practically assured that we'd not be able to make our initial flight ... which would also prevent us from making our connecting flight out of Houston in route to San Diego.

— OR—

Option B: Call customer service and inform them that we are in route to Houston to catch our connecting flight from Houston to San Diego. The highways to Houston were in much better shape than the Interstate to Austin. However, one airline representative informed us that we couldn't just skip ahead to our connecting flight in another city unless it had been cleared by customer service and that, in many cases, they don't allow it.

Despite our poor odds, we chose option A. Somehow, we needed to trek over icy roads to Austin to catch an 11:30 a.m. flight. Without ice, this would've been no problem, since the trip usually only takes an hour and a half.

But we had no idea the trip was going to take us nearly as long as it did, nor did we know it would entail half the road rage it entailed. Maybe something about the icy roads that day had everyone a little on edge.

After having driven just twenty minutes going fifteen miles per hour and seeing half the city's vehicle population in the ditch, I opted to try the access road rather than the backed-up interstate. It became apparent that the maximum speed limit our car could go without spinning out of control was around seventeen miles per hour. So we were perfectly content to drive our Miss Daisy-like speed of around fifteen.

About a mile down the access road, a truck traveling between forty-five and fifty-five miles per hour ran up from behind us, tailgating our car. I looked in the rear-view mirror, and truck guy was visibly angry with us for traveling so slowly. The friends who accompanied me on this trip had also felt the car lose control around seventeen miles per hour and were happy to hang around fifteen miles per hour. But, this has to be one of the things I love about road rage: It's being able to see a single driver raise his arms and yell in a vehicle, without anyone available to hear. It seems like that's actually the point of yelling—so the person you are yelling at can actually hear what you're saying and feel the animosity. All I could see, though, were his arms banging on the steering wheel. Odd.

At this point, all truck-guy was angry over was the speed at which we were traveling. His next available opportunity, though, truck-guy shifted into high gear to pass us, and when he moved out beside our car, he extended a greeting. I waved at him, and he became even angrier.

Now, I've seen numerous forms of road rage. I've seen extended fingers, tailgating, and even the finger outside the window. But until that day, I had never seen someone stop their vehicle and get out on a public access road, on which the speed limit was fifty-five miles per hour. Truck-guy pulled around our car and immediately slowed his truck to a halt. He stepped out and continued yelling things—thankfully, my mother was not in earshot of such words. He walked over a few feet from my driver's side window, and I began thinking, "Wow. I can't say I've ever experienced this before. Where is my journal? Because this experience really requires journaling."

I know I have Kung Fu-like moves and cat-like reflexes, so lucky for him, I stayed in the car. A good sensei will instruct his pupils not to flaunt their abilities, and I must admit that I've learned well. It was only after I positioned the car as though to pull around his that he jumped back in his truck and drove off.

Traveling at a steady fifteen miles per hour, we finally arrived in Austin five hours later and missed our flight.

Now, outside of our original two options, there were still other unknowns as well! Once we arrived in Austin, could those Austin flights have become delayed due to inclement weather? Sure. Or, could the weather take a turn for the worse between Waco and Houston, negating *anything* customer service had said? Sure, that's a possibility as well. In other words, this decision was loaded with about as many unknowns as the decisions we make in real life. Life in general is as unpredictable as the weather.

After some discussions and research, we obviously made the decision to travel to Austin, encountering road rage and all. But we made the decision with limited information, and at every turn in life, this is who we are. We are humans making human decisions with limited information. We are not God making God-like decisions with total information. Yet, at times, we approach God, and what we're really wanting is to transcend our humanness. We'd rather not encounter catastrophe, so we hope God will be the variable that saves us from it.

There will be several times along our journeys when we'll make some good, solid decisions based on:

- The amount of knowledge we have before us
- The amount of experiences we've had in our past
- The type of counsel we've received from others

But we must keep in mind that a good decision will not always reap a happy ending. There are perfectly good decisions we make in life with the amount of information we have, but those decisions will not always turn out as we hoped. With that in mind, let's go back and answer our initial question, then. Even though my relationship with that particular girl ended in breakup, was dating her a bad decision? No. After the breakup, I immediately thought, "What a mistake! What a waste of time! I spent a year and a half of my life just to eliminate one more girl from the sea of marriage possibilities. What a waste of time. What a mistake." In retrospect, though, I don't regret dating her at all. Why? Because I also took responsibility for my decision and allowed that experience to refine my search for God's will in choosing my mate for life. As I look at the road behind me, I can see that she was much closer to the type of girl I wanted to marry than my very first girlfriend. And still, I left that relationship thinking, "The type of girl I need as a mate for life needs to have this, this, and this, rather than this, this, and this ..."

Now, what would have been a poor decision? A poor decision would have been to turn right around and six months later begin dating the same type of girl! Or, a bad decision would have been to never get out of the relationship in the first place, even though I knew deep down that something was not right.

We will all have relationship experiences or job experiences in life, and the experiences that end up unhappily don't have to be a waste of time! They're only a waste of time if we don't allow those experiences to mold and shape who we are, who we are becoming, and where we need to be in the future. In the end,

I've taken responsibility for the paths I've chosen and the people I've dated. And I took responsibility for dating one particular girl seventeen months, sixteen of which were probably too long.

Thankfully, those previous relationships truly refined my search for a wife, as I'm happily married today. But as you can see, it wasn't for lack of heartbreak. I've had my fair share of failed relationships—or failed treasure map attempts. And while Jen and I enjoy a most fulfilling life together, our wedding day certainly wasn't the arrival point, the X on the map, or the final destination—three kids later, it undoubtedly looks like the beginning of another adventure. And a wild adventure at that. Let's not let images of formulas, blueprints, and treasure maps shape our understanding of God's will. Instead, let's let images of discipleship, fatherhood, and kingdom reframe our approach to God's will so that we see life with God as an adventure ... an adventure that will produce a person of character, sacrifice, and faith—all in all, a person like Jesus.

1. Haddon Robinson in Gary Friesen's *Decision Making and The Will of God* (Multnomah Publishers, Sisters, Oregon: 1980) p. 13.

APPENDICES
CONFUSING PASSAGES

PROVERBS 3:5-6
ROMANS 8:28
JEREMIAH 29:11

My aim in this final section is to address three specific passages—maybe the predominant, most oft-quoted passages—that relate to the subject of God's will. While I hope to engage these passages in an intellectually credible way, my aim is not to exhaustively exegete these specific verses. Certainly, there are entire books devoted to each one on the shelf. Rather, my aim is to communicate that, as a pastor, I *have* considered these passages in light of the direction this book has taken. And what follows is my understanding of each one. Though my aim is not to write volumes on each passage, I hope it becomes evident that each one is approached thoughtfully and contextually.

APPENDIX A
STRAIGHT PATHS?

CONFUSING PASSAGE: PROVERBS 3:5-6

"Trust in the LORD with all your heart, and do not rely on your own insight. In all your ways acknowledge him, and he will make straight your paths." Proverbs 3:5-6 NRSV

The Christian Scriptures are made up of a beautiful mosaic of narratives, poetry, and teachings written by a vast number of authors and spanning thousands of years. From Genesis to Revelation, the various books and letters of the Bible were originally written in rich languages that modern-day English can't always adequately explain.

In my own journey over the years, my love and respect for this sacred text has greatly deepened—but not without struggle. Anyone who has approached the ancient Scriptures honestly, thoughtfully, and deliberately has found him or herself with mixed responses—amazed, awakened, confused, stressed, motivated, mystified, troubled, overjoyed ...

If you were raised in an environment where scripture passages were quoted at will, can you remember the first time you encountered a *different meaning* for a commonly quoted verse? I can. It was a shock to the system. For instance, the first time I discovered the true meaning of the word "repent," it was both shocking and liberating—shocking because at some level, I felt I had been duped by those who demanded that following Jesus would entail uncontrollable sobbing, but liberating because though I have chosen to live my life in the ways of Jesus, I've never really sobbed about it.

And still, I have "repented," because "repent" comes from the root word *metanoia*—*meta* meaning "again" and *noia* meaning "to think." *Noia* comes from a root word that has to do with cognition or thinking. So literally, "repent" simply means "to think again." But usually, given the context in which it's used in the New Testament, I'd say that "repent" has this sort of connotation: It's like, if I were on my way to see a particular movie, and I called a friend who I knew had seen it and asked, "What did you think of _____? Was it good?" And they said, "Absolutely not! It was one of the dumbest movies I've seen in a while. In fact, all the funniest parts were in the previews." Then, I'd probably respond by "repenting" of what I had originally intended to do. I'd respond by not seeing that particular movie.

Now, given our understanding of the language, a good rendering of "repent" would be to "reconsider the direction you're headed." Or, in light of its typical usage in the New Testament, it means "to reconsider your entire way of living." Come to think of it, in my own life, repentance takes place fairly often. Even on a weekly basis!

Every single passage of scripture from Genesis to Revelation was embedded within a specific setting with its own language, values, problems, and audience. To swiftly uproot it and set it back down in the twenty-first century without a single thought to its own setting is to do violence to this sacred text.

So, how could a passage mean anything other than what you've thought it meant in the past? For two reasons: Either the passage is explained in view of the original language in which it was written (Hebrew or Greek), or the passage is explained in view of its historical background. Herein lies the number one reason our sacred text is treated so recklessly in today's world—blatant disregard of the language and historical context in which it was written.

Paul's letter to the Philippians was not written by a Middle-Eastern fellow with an English lexicon in hand from a dimly lit table in the back corner of Starbuck's on the corner of Broadway and Shiloh Road in Chicago last week. And if, in fact, it wasn't, then does that make any difference in the way we approach the letter to the Philippians? I'd think that in the very least, it would demand that we approach scripture with a greater sense of humility about the very words we are interpreting.

Instinctively, every time we approach the Scriptures, we ought to be wondering these sorts of things (even if we don't know the answer):

- Who was this author writing to, and why was this letter, book, or Gospel being written?

- What issues, problems, or dilemmas were facing this community (Corinthian, Galatian, Ephesian, etc.) that necessitated this letter, book, or Gospel?

- Could there be any language barriers in this passage between our English language and the original Hebrew or Greek?

In fact, this ought to be a natural rite of passage within our apprenticeship to Jesus. Just as our view of God should look different from when we were three, so should our approach to scripture. Our understanding of God at twenty-five should certainly be more thoughtful and intentional than at five. Likewise, our approach to scripture should be more thoughtful and deliberate at twenty-five, as opposed to five. If our apprenticeship to Jesus is ever going to move into full adulthood, then we must strive to approach scripture on its terms, not ours. With this in mind, let's look at the first passage in scripture that has been referenced frequently in conversations about God's will:

> "Trust in the Lord with all your heart,
> And do not rely on your own insight.
> In all your ways acknowledge him,
> And he will make straight your paths."
> (Proverbs 3:5-6 NRSV)

At first glance, some will read Proverbs 3:5-6 and be genuinely moved to acknowledge God in every aspect of their lives. Others will read these two verses in light of our journey over the past several chapters and immediately raise a few questions. For example, some could read "do not rely on your own insight" and imagine this passage as encouraging its hearers to shun intelligence and even the advice of others in lieu of solely basing one's decision-making on an inner dialogue with God. Or, some could read "he will make straight your paths" and wonder if acknowledging God will actually remove all obstacles from their journey in life.

If either of these options is the case, then this would obviously run against the grain of previous chapters. Namely, some people could very well leave this passage and encourage Lone Ranger decision-making: "Don't listen to anyone around you. Only listen to God, because the Scriptures do say, "Trust in the Lord with ALL YOUR HEART." In fact, the use of your brains is against the will of God, because more often than not, God will NOT make any sense at all."

Any individual could leave Proverbs 3:5-6 with this approach to God's will:

- If you want to discover God's will for your life, listen only to God and not to those around you (verse 5).

- God's direction for your life will usually fly in the face of common sense (verse 5).

- If you acknowledge God in everything you do, then you'll be safe from all bad things in life, and your journey will be a smooth, carefree road (verse 6).

However, let's look at this passage a bit closer. Verses 1-4 say:

> "My child, do not forget my teaching,
> but let your heart keep my commandments;
> for length of days and years of life
> and abundant welfare they will give you.
> Do not let loyalty and faithfulness forsake you;
> bind them around your neck,
> write them on the tablet of your heart.
> So you will find favor and good repute
> in the sight of God and of people."
> (Proverbs 3:1-4 NRSV)

The overall thrust of the chapter beginning in verse 1 has to do with character issues. Will you be a person of loyalty, love, and faithfulness (verse 3)? Will you be a person who actually puts to practice the very teachings you've been taught (verse 1)? Will you be a reputable person for living a life of integrity (verse 4)? In fact, the instruction to "not rely on your own insight" follows the same vein of "forming a person of character" that's found not only throughout chapter 3, but throughout the entire book of Proverbs.

In verse 7, the chapter continues, "Do not be wise in your own eyes; fear the Lord, and turn away from evil." A major thrust in the book of Proverbs is the eternal value of *wisdom*. In fact, Proverbs falls within a group of books in the Old Testament known as "Wisdom Literature." Ironically, people who are truly wise know that there are limits to their intelligence; therefore, they would never assume that their own limited understanding of life will reap "the straight path." In other words, Proverbs 3:5-6 isn't an encouragement toward impulsive or Lone Ranger decision-making. Any person of wisdom knows the value of consulting God, friends, and family members in the decision-making process.

THROUGH THE LENS OF JESUS

Then, here's where I begin to struggle with the passage. I think it's important that when we approach scripture, we strive to be fully present with the text. Rather than glossing over any potential problem areas, we wrestle with it, even when passages make us uncomfortable or confused.

The next thing we notice in this particular passage is that so much of verses 5 and 6 lead up to this word "*straight.*" An NAS Hebrew lexicon translates this word several ways: "*to be right, straight, level, upright, just, lawful, smooth.*"[1] I even noticed another translator who used two interchangeable words for "straight" paths—"smooth" or "successful." Now, in light of previous chapters, this ought to raise some questions. Namely, does that mean that the more we acknowledge God in every aspect of our lives, the fewer obstacles we'll encounter? Not hardly.

There is a struggle we should all be aware of in the Old Testament. And if we're not aware of this tension, it could and will create disastrous effects in our relationship with God. If we're going to approach the Scriptures thoughtfully and intentionally, we should openly discuss these tension areas. The tension is this: In Deuteronomy, the mindset about relating with God that's pervasive communicates, "If I follow God and act in accordance with the Jewish Law, then God will bless me through material means and remove hindrances from my life." Hindrances could be enemies, illness, poverty, or day-to-day difficulties.

Then, within the Old Testament itself, you begin to see an inner dialogue take place between this Deuteronomic mindset (following God = financial blessing and easy road) and some of the Wisdom Literature. In particular, Job struggles with this Deuteronomic tradition, as he lives a faithful life, but sees his family and possessions obliterated! And by the time Jesus comes on the scene in the New Testament, you really see some distinctions between Deuteronomy and the letters of Paul and other letters in the New Testament. Certainly, the early followers of Jesus didn't have the expectation that following Him would entail an easy life. For instance, Luke 9 says, "Then he said to them all, 'If any want to become my followers, let them deny themselves and take up their cross daily and follow me. For those who want to save their life will lose it, and those who lose their life for my sake will save it. What does it profit them if they gain the whole world, but lose or forfeit themselves?" (Luke 9:23-25 NRSV). And in I Peter, the Scriptures say, "Now who will harm you if you are eager to do what is good? But even if you do suffer for doing what is right, you are blessed" (1 Peter 3:13-14 NRSV).

In fact, whatever struggles I encounter in scripture, my general rule of thumb is to try to look at that particular passage in light of Jesus. I place Jesus at the center of the Scriptures and try to understand Genesis through Revelation in light of Him, His life, and His ministry. That doesn't mean I never encounter confusion or difficulties. It just means that in Jesus, I have a tangible person to look to in trying to center my life. In light of Him, I can then try to answer important questions like, "How do I define success?" Or, "What might 'a straight path' look like to Jesus?" And in light of Him, I simply come back to this: *A successful life is a transformed life.* People today could very well be rich or poor. The wealthy could have become wealthy by malpractice, and the poor could have become poor by being lazy. Or the wealthy could have become wealthy due to wise decision-making, and the poor could have become poor due to oppression. Either way, you can't judge a book by its cover. However, in light of Jesus, I do know this—that a life transformed in the ways of Jesus is a successful life and is most likely to experience life in the way it was meant to be lived.

So in light of Jesus and the context of Proverbs, I would interpret Proverbs 3:5-6 as saying, "Trust God with all that you have—your mind, your heart, and your soul. Don't base your life and future only on your own limited intelligence and experiences. Instead, recognize the reality of God in every aspect of your life, and you will find yourself on the path of transformation, which leads to fulfillment."

---

1. Brown, Driver, Briggs, Gesenius Lexicon, *www.biblestudytools.net/Lexicons Hebrew.*

APPENDIX B
DOES EVERYTHING ACTUALLY HAPPEN FOR A REASON?

CONFUSING PASSAGE: ROMANS 8:28

"We know that all things work together for good for those who love God, who are called according to His purpose."
Romans 8:28 NRSV

There is perhaps no more redemptive verse in all of scripture than Romans 8:28. For when our lives have come unraveled, this is the passage to embrace. And, unfortunately, this is also the passage that's done quite a bit of damage through the years when referenced by well-intending individuals who chose to quote it at the most in-opportune times. For instance, imagine how this verse sounds when quoted to someone who's just experienced the unexpected death of a family member or close friend. Or when a husband and father of four has just lost his job with very little in savings and zero alternatives. Or when a fifteen-year-old girl has just been diagnosed with a brain tumor.

There are, in fact, times in life when Romans 8:28 can evoke
animosity rather than hope for the future, because some Bible
translations present the passage from a different angle. The New
American Standard translates Romans 8:28 in this way: "And
we know that *God causes all things* to work together for good
to those who love God, to those who are called according to
His purpose" (emphasis mine). In other words, the passage has a
different feel because, in the verse, God has been placed before
"all things," rather than "all things" being placed before God.
Naturally, people who have found themselves in a place of crisis
won't need any help attributing their current predicament to
God. They'll be more prone to hearing the passage read, "And
we know that *God causes all things*" and stop there. Immediately,
their anger will be stirred, because God is the one who's just
taken the life of their family member or fired them from a job
or placed a tumor in their brain.

In fact, one of the more popular translations of Romans 8:28
could easily be equated with folklore. "Folklore," or "folk theology," is a term a friend of mine uses to describe an age-old
phrase that many people say all the time but no one knows
from where it came. He says there are all sorts of phrasings
and anecdotes people use today in casual conversation that, for
them, function as scripture even though they're not actually
found in the Bible. Tragically enough, they've just been assumed.
The particular folklore reading of Romans 8:28 might then be,
"Everything happens for a reason."

But did you know that "everything happens for a reason" isn't
a scripture verse? It's not a proverb or a psalm, and it's not an
admonition from Ecclesiastes. And in this respect, it can take on
even more authority than scripture itself precisely because it's
found on the lips of people inside *and* outside the Church. It's
global, and yet it's not actually written down anywhere, alleviating it from actually being examined. It's practically assumed by

all as unwavering truth—that is, until you find yourself trying to make sense of unspeakable tragedy or until you begin applying this "creed" to every detail of your life. So, unemployed fathers of four and cancerous fifteen-year-old girls, "everything happens for a reason," so try to figure it out.

A further look at Romans 8:28 might render a different translation, though. First, let's back up and look at the bigger picture of where Paul has been headed in chapter 8. In most translations, this specific verse falls within a section of verses beginning in verse 18. "I consider that the sufferings of this present time are not worth comparing with the glory about to be revealed to us" (Romans 8:18 NRSV). The subject matter Paul is dealing with here is that of "sufferings," times of despair all of us encounter at some time or another. It's almost as if you can hear the question being posed, "So what do we make of all the times in our lives when we encounter suffering, tragedy, and despair? What do we make of distresses, losses, or failures that overtake our lives, often times unexpectedly?"

Then, in verses 26 and 27, a beautiful passage is offered that communicates the Spirit's action during these times. The Message recounts these verses in this way: "Meanwhile, the moment we get tired in the waiting, God's Spirit is right alongside helping us along. If we don't know how or what to pray, it doesn't matter. He does our praying in and for us, making prayer out of our wordless sighs, our aching groans. He knows us far better than we know ourselves, knows our pregnant condition, and keeps us present before God" (Romans 8:26-27).

It's in this context of suffering, then, that verse 28 is found. Again, there are some differences among translations about which phrase comes first in the sentence—"God" or "all things." But whatever the case, I think the intended meaning remains the same. It's important that we take the entire verse in view. To stop short of the last word would create an entirely different message. We can't stop at "*God causes all things.*" Nor can we stop at "*all things work together for good.*"

There are many, many intelligent people who firmly believe that God does in fact cause all things to happen in today's world, even tragic situations. And they haven't come to this conclusion flippantly. Many believe this to be true after diligent study of the Scriptures. However, that is not my belief. I believe tragedy, chaos, and disease are natural consequences of the Fall when humankind was given freedom of choice. Yet, no matter who you are or where your theology stands, all people who strive to thoughtfully deal with God and life are forced to live within the tension of God's providence and a chaotic world. Still, no matter where you stand on the issue, Romans 8:28 still proves to be a redemptive passage: "We know that all things work together for good ..." After reading the passage, a few pivotal questions to ask would be:

- What are "all things"?
- What kind of "good" is Paul talking about?
- Who is this "good" being created for?

What are "all things"? Again, does this statement mean that God is currently causing all things that happen in the world? No. Within the context of chapter 8, Paul is referring to all of our experiences of suffering, disappointment, loss, and failure in this world. In other words, we live in a fallen world where poor, unethical, impaired decisions are made. We live in a world where no one is exempt from illness and disease. BUT, *in all these things*, God can create good out of disaster.

So, what is this "good"? Does this mean that if I consistently pray, God will automatically alleviate disaster, heal disease, and create tranquility around me? No, although that could very well happen. God's definition of "good" is often different than ours. Previously in Romans, Paul states, "And not only that, but we also boast in our sufferings, knowing that suffering produces endurance, and endurance produces character, and character produces hope, and hope does not disappoint us, because God's love has been poured out into our hearts through the Holy Spirit that has been given us" (Romans 5:3-5 NRSV).

"Good" does not always mean "good" by our standards. Instead, "good" by God's standards has to do with the continual process of becoming a learner of Christ where our lives are being formed into people of humility, compassion, self-control, respect, patience, contentment, etc. It has to do with learning the very best way to live. If we open our eyes and our hearts during the most difficult times in our lives, then even in those times, God can bring about some of the most beautiful things within and around us.

And for whom is this "good" being created? Does the "good" just happen on its own? It explicitly takes place *"for those who love God, who are called according to His purpose."* In other words, this "good" happens within those who have clearly and intentionally set their lives on the path toward becoming a whole-life learner of Jesus. Ninety-nine percent of the time, it doesn't just happen. Life transformation isn't an accident. It's a deliberate attempt by those who love God to allow every experience into the interior of their lives, and in the process, hopefully, see God's redemptive activity: friendships restored, renewed reliance on God, an awakening to the beauty of life, clarity of purpose, renewed compassion for others ...

So in light of chapter 8, I would interpret Romans 8:28 as saying this: "Disappointment, failure, and suffering are simply facts of life. But for those who are actively following God, He can turn disappointment and tragedy into new life."

APPENDIX C
SHOULDN'T JEREMIAH
BE GIVEN A VOICE?

CONFUSING PASSAGE: JEREMIAH 29:11

"For surely, I know the plans I have for you, says the Lord, plans for your welfare and not for harm, to give you a future with hope." Jeremiah 29:11 NRSV

So God does in fact have an individual blueprint for our lives? We've been discussing all this time about the lack of any formulated plans, treasure maps, or recipes. But it says so right there, "*I know the* plans *I have for you ...*" This must be just the thing God references when we are requesting direction at ages twelve, seventeen, twenty-two, thirty ...

Again, if we are going to move on to approaching scripture as thoughtfully and responsibly as possible, we should instinctively be wondering these sorts of things (even if we don't know the answer):

- What were the circumstances that necessitated Jeremiah writing these very words? What was the historical setting in which these words were written?

- Do any language barriers exist between the Hebrew language (used in the Old Testament) and our English language today?

- How does this verse fall within the wider scope of chapter 29?

If the prophet Jeremiah were to sit in on a conversation at a local restaurant today, would he protest the way his words were quoted? Would he say, "No, no, no. That has nothing to do with what I was saying when I was saying it"? I think it's this sort of respect with which we should approach the Scriptures if we are going to treat it with the sense of sacredness it deserves.

Some could very well argue, "Yes, but at some point after reading the Scriptures, we apply our readings *to today*." And I agree, but it's at that very place that we either choose responsibility or recklessness. When moving to the place of applying our readings to today, we'll either take an imaginative step in full view of the verse's context, or we'll take an irresponsible leap over skyscrapers and football fields. So, in trying to interpret Jeremiah 29:11, let's try to pull a chair up to the table for Jeremiah. It seems he should be given a voice in this conversation. Let's do our part in trying to listen ...

For the Jewish people, land was everything. Jerusalem was the capital of the Jewish people and understood as the residence of YHWH God. The temple Solomon built existed in Jerusalem. But in 597 B.C., the Babylonians attacked Jerusalem, and many of the Jews were taken as captives and deported to Babylon. This community of people who had been exiled to Babylon was the intended audience of chapter 29. "These are the words of the letter that the prophet Jeremiah sent from Jerusalem to the remaining elders among the exiles, and to the priests, the prophets, and all the people, whom Nebuchadnezzar had taken into exile from Jerusalem to Babylon." (Jeremiah 29:1 NRSV)

While in Babylon, those in exile wanted desperately to return home to Jerusalem. This was a day and age where false prophets were frequent and many were probably consulting dream interpreters in the hopes they'd be told, "Now is the time. Rise up against Babylon in holy war." The problem was, some really were prophesying and divining against Jeremiah's instruction. We don't know exactly what they were saying, but we know it was the opposite of what Jeremiah called for—a time of peace:

> Build houses and live in them; plant gardens and eat what they produce. Take wives and have sons and daughters; take wives for your sons, and give your daughters in marriage, that they may bear sons and daughters; multiply there, and do not decrease. But seek the welfare of the city where I have sent you into exile, and pray to the Lord on its behalf, for in its welfare you will find your welfare (Jeremiah 29: 5-7 NRSV).

Jeremiah rejected the instructions of these false prophets and diviners: "For thus says the Lord of hosts, the God of Israel: Do not let the prophets and diviners who are among you deceive you, and do not listen to the dreams that they dream, for it is a lie that they are prophesying to you in my name; I did not send them, says the Lord" (Jeremiah 29:8-9 NRSV). And in verse 10, Jeremiah explains precisely why he rejected the instructions of these prophets:

> "For thus says the Lord: Only when Babylon's seventy years are completed will I visit you, and I will fulfill to

you my promise and bring you back to this place."
(Jeremiah 29:10 NRSV)

In fact, this chapter provides greater proof that Jeremiah was a
true prophet! Chapter 29 was written to the 597 B.C. exiles.
Many of them wanted to wage holy war and return home to
Jerusalem; but if they were to reject the command of God, they
would enjoy only a brief time of peace. In 586 B.C., the Babylonians returned to Jerusalem and, this time, completely obliterated the city and the Temple.

In other words, if the exiled Jews had followed the instruction
of the false prophets and diviners, they would have been killed.
On the other hand, Jeremiah voiced the command of YHWH
to live peacefully in Babylon for seventy years, a period of time
outlasting the destruction of the Temple in 586 B.C. However,
in the eyes of the exiled, what God was calling them to do was
extraordinary. He was commanding them to:

- Abandon their plans of escape,
- Live in what they thought was literally "God-forsaken"
  land, and
- Live there for *seventy years*.

How could this be hopeful for an exiled Jew? After seventy
years, most of the ones who heard this command would be
dead or pretty close to it! So where's the hope in that?

The hope YHWH speaks of is found in full view of the destruction of the Temple in 586 B.C., "For surely, I know the
plans I have for you, says the Lord, plans for your welfare and
not for harm, to give you a future and a hope" (Jeremiah 29:11
NRSV). Literally, the hope YHWH speaks of is:

- A time of protection and peace,

- A future, *literally* grandchildren, great-grandchildren, great-great-grandchildren, etc., and
- God's presence (even in Babylon) and His response to prayer (verses 12–14).

For just a moment, let's consider this word "future" found in verse 11. Given the context of the entire chapter and its historical setting, "future" means grandkids. "Future" literally means *future.* "Future" is not a metaphorical term; "future" has a face. If the exiled Jews were to follow the instruction of the false prophets, there would be no future. Their existence would be wiped out in 586 B.C. trying to protect the Temple. There would be no grandchildren or great-grandchildren to enjoy God's promise of restoration after seventy years. So "future" has to do with descendants who would come after them in future years because they chose to listen to God's command and not return to Jerusalem prematurely.

Now after considering Jeremiah's audience, their newfound homeland, the problem of false prophets, and the destruction of the Temple in 586 B.C., how does Jeremiah 29:11 sound, and does that have anything to do with how we interpret the passage today? My opinion is that it should, and it should profoundly.

The first time I reconsidered Jeremiah 29:11 in light of its context, it felt different to me, but I couldn't exactly articulate why. So I began comparing how I've typically used and understood this word—"plans"—with how it is used in verse 11 to see if the two lined up. In other words, my aim wasn't to extract "plans" out of its setting in the sixth century B.C., but to see if my understanding matched up. And here's what I realized ...

I traced my usage of "plans" back to a particular church billboard I referenced earlier in the book, a large billboard on which was depicted a few men in hard hats examining a large architectural blueprint. In big block letters, the caption read, "Discover God's Plan for Your Life"—with the church's information and gathering times below.

In truth, I've got as much experience in architecture as George Costanza, but I *have* seen a set of blueprints in my life. And I know the intricacies they define. Buildings and homes stand or fall by these details. In the same way, if God were to have a blueprint—a *plan*—of my life, I've always thought it to be broken down into years, months, days, minutes, and seconds. And it would be in my best interest, then, to follow this plan. In fact, the success of my life depends on how well I execute this plan. This is my American, twenty-first-century understanding of "plan."

Verse 11's use of "plans" seems a bit different, though. First of all, I can't help but see this as a *corporate* plan rather than an *individual* plan. That is, Jeremiah 29 seems as though it's aimed at a large group of people rather than an isolated individual.

Secondly, it does have a sense of foresight to it in that God commands the exiled Jews to reside in Babylon for seventy years. However, its foresight seems as though it's directed at how this corporate group of people should spend their next seventy years (building houses, planting gardens, having kids, etc.), not where an individual person should take his or her next step in college, career, dating, or relationships. In other words, the foresight involved doesn't seem as though it's broken-down for individual Jewish exiles in years, months, days, and seconds. And it doesn't involve a specific job that each individual exiled Jew should take up.

In fact, what does God instruct them to do?

Build houses and live in them; plant gardens and eat what they produce. Take wives and have sons and daughters; take wives for your sons, and give your daughters in marriage, that they may bear sons and daughters; multiply there, and do not decrease. But seek the welfare of the city where I have sent you into exile, and pray to the Lord on its behalf, for in its welfare you will find your welfare. (Jeremiah 29:5-7 NRSV)

So the "plan" in verse 11 seems to be a corporate plan aimed at the physical survival and restoration of the exiled Jews, not so much an individual plan aimed at how well twenty-first-century Christians execute every decision every second of the day. Verse 11 doesn't seem as though it's about God treating humans like machinery and designing individual lives for the purpose of performance or for the sole purpose of arriving at a final destination. And it doesn't sound like an individual plan aimed at achievement.

In the end, it's my opinion that when Jeremiah 29:11 is placed within the context of sixth century B.C., it holds little resemblance to its usage twenty-six hundred years later. In light of its own setting, I'd translate Jeremiah 29:11 like ... well ... I guess I'd leave it just like it is: "For surely, I know the plans I have for you, says the Lord, plans for your welfare and not for harm, to give you a future with hope" ... minus the billboard.

[RELEVANTBOOKS]